RS-232 SIMPLIFIED

Everything You Need to Know
About Connecting,
Interfacing, and
Troubleshooting Peripheral
Devices

RS-232 SIMPLIFIED
Everything You Need to Know About Connecting, Interfacing, and Troubleshooting Peripheral Devices

BYRON W. PUTMAN

Computer Facilities and Communications
University of California, Berkeley

Prentice-Hall, Inc., Englewood Cliffs, New Jersey 07632

Library of Congress Cataloging-in-Publication Data

PUTMAN, BYRON W.
    RS-232 simplified.

    Includes index.
    1. Computer interfaces—Standards—United States.
    2. Computer interfaces.   I. Title.
    TK7887.5.P87 1987   004.6'2   86-18701
    ISBN   0-13-783507-8
    ISBN   0-13-783499-3 (pbk.)

Editorial/production supervision
and interior design: *Theresa A. Soler*
Cover design: *Photo Plus Art*
Manufacturing buyer: *Carol Bystrom*

Printed in the United States of America
10   9   8   7   6   5   4   3   2   1

ISBN   0-13-783507-8
ISBN   0-13-783499-3   {PBK.}   025

Prentice-Hall International (UK) Limited, *London*
Prentice-Hall of Australia Pty. Limited, *Sydney*
Prentice-Hall Canada Inc., *Toronto*
Prentice-Hall Hispanoamericana, S.A., *Mexico*
Prentice-Hall of India Private Limited, *New Delhi*
Prentice-Hall of Japan, Inc., *Tokyo*
Prentice-Hall of Southeast Asia Pte. Ltd., *Singapore*
Editora Prentice-Hall do Brasil, Ltda., *Rio de Janeiro*

*To those courageous individuals
who have taken a break-out box in hand
and made an interface work.*

Contents

7 DESIGNING AND CONSTRUCTING RS-232 INTERFACE CABLES   91

8 TROUBLESHOOTING INTERFACE MALFUNCTIONS   111

Preface

It's impossible to estimate the number of times I've been called by a friend or a friend of a friend with a panicked voice and shattered nerves relating a story of woe concerning an RS-232 terminal, microcomputer, printer, or modem that was guaranteed to be compatible with their system but just didn't seem to work. Often they place the blame on themselves, stating that they're just too stupid to understand the manufacturer's documentation. All they want to do is to connect the devices together and have them work. Is that too much to ask?

Assembling a particular computer system is a fairly straightforward process. The problems start when one wants to venture beyond packaged systems and purchase third-parity peripherals. Typically the salesperson will assure the user that the particular device will function without modification on his or her present system—after all, its RS-232 compatible!

The RS-232 serial interface standard was drafted in the 1960s by the Electronics Industries Association. It was designed to create a hardware independent environment between terminals, modems, and computers. In the 20 years since the inception of RS-232 computer hardware has evolved at an exponential rate, but the original standard has changed very little. The use of long-since archaic terms (such as "data set") is extremely confusing to the interfacing novice. This leaves a tremendous gap between the intended application of RS-232 and the actual devices that are now standard components in computer systems.

The single greatest obstacle encountered while interfacing RS-232 peripherals is the fact that the standard is written in such a way that almost every manufacturer interprets and implements the interface connection in a slightly unique manner. RS-232 is a nonstandard standard, vulnerable to modifications and customization.

The objective of this book is to illustrate RS-232 in the light of modern peripheral devices. It is not a theoretical treatise on formal serial interface design. After completing this book the user should be able to correctly setup any RS-232 device, and design and construct custom interface cables.

This book is designed to fulfill the needs of a wide variety of people, from professional electronics technicians and ADP analysts, to the microcomputer hobbyist and the local office "microconsultant." It is also suitable for a one-quarter or one-semester course on serial interfacing.

The only prerequisite required for the successful reading of this book is simply a strong interest in interfacing computers and peripherals.

Chapter 1 is an introduction to digital electronics and the binary number system. This chapter is provided to introduce nonhardware people to the realm of TTL and digital levels. It should be considered completely optional and can be skipped with absolutely no adverse effects.

Chapter 2 examines the ASCII code with emphasis on the difference between control codes and printable ASCII characters.

Chapter 3 analyzes the RS-232 standard from a pragmatic point of view. DTEs and DCEs, the DB-25 pinout, and RS-232 voltage/logic levels are discussed.

Chapter 4 details the structure of the bit stream as it propagates along the transmission line. The concepts of framing information and parity checking are considered in detail. The standard RS-232 line-driver and line-receiver ICs are also examined.

Chapter 5 investigates the difference between standard RS-232 terminals and the video monitors employed in microcomputer systems. Terminal setup parameters, the concepts of programming terminals and terminal drivers, and terminal emulation with microcomputers are examined.

Chapter 6 describes the setup and applications of the most popular RS-232 peripherals: modems, printers, and print buffers are described.

Chapter 7 puts it all together. Using the expertise developed in the previous chapters, the techniques of designing interface cables with the aid of manufacturer's documentation and empirically creating cables with a break-out box are detailed. The construction of RS-232 cables and useful utility devices are also described.

Chapter 8 attacks the question of what to do when two devices refuse to communicate. Common symptoms and solutions, and the use of digital multimeters and oscilloscopes are discussed.

ACKNOWLEDGMENTS

I would like to thank Carroll Touch and Okidata, Division of Oki Amoncia, Inc. for providing selected illustrations.

Byron W. Putman

OTHER PRENTICE-HALL BOOKS BY THIS AUTHOR

DIGITAL ELECTRONICS: Theory, Applications, and Troubleshooting

DIGITAL AND MICROPROCESSOR ELECTRONICS: Theory, Applications, and Troubleshooting

RS-232 SIMPLIFIED

Everything You Need to Know About Connecting, Interfacing, and Troubleshooting Peripheral Devices

1

Digital Electronics

and

Computer Systems

1.1 ANALOG COMPUTATION

Let's consider a simple experiment where we add the integers 5 and 3 using an electronic circuit to accomplish the actual calculation. The most intuitive method is to represent each number with an analogous voltage level. The number 5 can be represented with a $+5$ V DC level and the number three, with a $+3$ V DC level.

Figure 1.1 is an elementary Op-amp adder circuit. The *wiper arm* on resistors R_1 and R_2 can be adjusted to produce any voltage between $+12$ V and -12 V. Voltage V_1 ($+5$ V) is summed with V_2 ($+3$ V), and the voltage analogous to the number 8 ($+8$ V) appears at V_{out}. We could easily verify the result of the addition with a *digital voltmeter* (DVM) or an oscilloscope.

Do not be concerned if you are not familiar with the Op-amp adder circuit in Figure 1.1. The critical concept here is that a numeric quantity can be represented with a voltage. That is, the magnitude of the voltages in Figure 1.1 are analogous to the numeric quantities that we wish to add.

To understand the limitations of such a method of addition, consider the addition of the fractional quantities 5.25 and 3.68. Again, we can represent each numeric quantity with a voltage level, but notice the added constraints on the system. All the electronic components in the circuit must not induce an error greater than 0.01 V. That also implies that the DVM or oscilloscope we use to obtain the result of the addition must be carefully calibrated and accurate to at least .01 V.

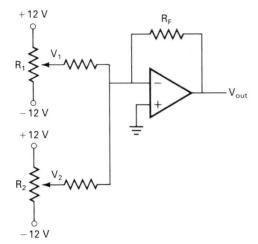

Figure 1.1 Adding two numbers with an electronic circuit.

What happens if

10 or 20 mV of noise are induced on the input or output voltages?

We need more than .01 V of precision?

We want to add numbers greater than $+12$ V or -12 V?

We need a different circuit for subtraction, multiplication, division, and other common math functions?

We want to "store" the result so it can be used with another operation or saved for future reference?

The previous addition example employed the use of *analog* circuits. In analog circuits a quantity is represented by an analogous voltage level. In Figure 1.1 either resistor could be adjusted to represent the infinite number of real numbers that exist between $+12$ and -12.

1.2 DIGITAL ELECTRONICS

The first computers were constructed from analog circuitry and operated in a similar (albeit much more complex) fashion to the example in Figure 1.1. The many problems and limitations entailed by using analog circuits for computation were largely overcome by the development of the modern *digital* circuit. In complete contrast to the analog circuits that we have just examined, only two voltage levels can exist in a digital circuit. Digital circuits can be grouped to represent any real number.

Figure 1.2 depicts the most common digital waveform—the *square wave*. Notice that a square wave has only two possible values, a high level and a low level. A

Figure 1.2   The square wave—a digital waveform.

practical understanding of the binary number system is required before we explore the concepts of electronically representing numeric quantities in a digital form.

People now use a *base*-10 (decimal) number system that is composed of 10 unique symbols. It is no coincidence that the number of digits in our number system and the number of digits on our hands are equal. Consider the simple process of counting. Starting with the first digit in our number system, we continue to increment the count until we have exhausted the supply of unique digits. A *carry* is then generated by incrementing the digit in the next significant column. The first column in a decimal number has a *place value* of 1. This means that each time the count is incremented, the number in column 1 is also incremented. The second column in a decimal number has a place value of 10; the number in the second column is incremented each 10 counts; the number in the third column is incremented every 100 counts; the fourth column, every 1000 counts. This pattern continues forever.

From our examination of the decimal number system, we can now make a general statement concerning place value. The place value of the first column of a number is equal to the base of the number system raised to the zero power. (For all number bases this value is 1.) The place value of the second column is equal to the base raised to the first power, the third column is equal to the base raised to the second power, and so on.

$$\text{Place value } = \text{ base }^{(\text{column number}-1)}$$

3rd Column	2nd Column	1st Column
base^2	base^1	base^0

How would we count if people had evolved with only six fingers? We would employ a number system with six unique digits:

$$0, 1, 2, 3, 4, 5$$

The place values in the base-6 system are powers of 6:

3rd Column	2nd Column	1st Column
$6^2 = 36$	$6^1 = 6$	$6^0 = 1$

Incrementing a count in base 6 gives 1, 2, 3, 4, 5, 10, ... The digit 6 does not exist; the generation of a carry after 5 produces 10 in base 6, which is equivalent to 6 in base 10.

1.3 THE BINARY NUMBER SYSTEM

Recall that digital circuits have only two possible voltage levels. The square wave in Figure 1.2 was described as a digital waveform. In our examination of how quantities are represented in digital circuits, we must consider which number system best describes digital electronics. Simply stated: How many fingers does a square wave have? The answer is two. The low portion of the square wave can represent one unique digit and the high part of the square wave, a second unique digit. The number system associated with digital circuits is called the *base-2*, or *binary*, number system.

Base 2 is the simplest of all number systems. It has only two unique digits, 0 and 1 (representing the two levels of the square wave). Figure 1.3 illustrates a counting table in binary. The value in the least significant column toggles each count. The value of the 2^1 column toggles every two counts; the next column, every four counts; and the last column, every eight counts.

Each column in a binary number is called a *bit*. This is contraction of the term *binary digit*. In the next chapter we study the *ASCII Code*, in which letters, numbers, punctuation marks, and other common symbols are each represented by unique patterns of bits. Our main interest here is to gain a practical understanding of binary numbers. If you already understand the binary number system, feel free to omit this section.

Figure 1.3 indicates that 4 bits can represent 16 unique numbers. The general formula

$$\text{Number of unique numbers} = 2^{\text{number of bits}}$$

relates bits and unique numbers. Thus 4 bits can represent 2^4 or 16, unique numbers, and 8 bits can represent 2^8 or 256, unique numbers. In digital electronics a group of 8 bits is called a *byte*, and a group of 4 bits is known as a *nibble*. A byte is the most common form of digital information. Within a computer's memory a byte can represent a letter, number, punctuation mark, quantity, address, or program instruction.

1.3.1 Binary Addition

The rules that govern binary addition are as simple as the binary number system itself. All that you must remember is:

$$
\begin{aligned}
0 + 0 &= 0 \\
1 + 0 &= 1 \\
1 + 1 &= 0 \quad \text{and a carry of 1} \\
1 + 1 + 1 &= 1 \quad \text{and a carry of 1}
\end{aligned}
$$

Consider the following examples:

Counting Table

	Comments:				Decimal equivalent
	2^3	2^2	2^1	2^0	
0000					0
+ __1					
0001				0 + 1 = 1	1
+ __1					
0010			0 + 1 = 1	1 + 1 = 0	2
+ __1					
0011				0 + 1 = 1	3
+ __1					
0100		0 + 1 = 1	1 + 1 = 0	1 + 1 = 0	4
+ __1					
0101				0 + 1 = 1	5
+ __1					
0110			0 + 1 = 1	1 + 1 = 0	6
+ __1					
0111				0 + 1 = 1	7
+ __1					
1000	0 + 1 = 1	1 + 1 = 0	1 + 1 = 0	1 + 1 = 0	8
+ __1					
1001				0 + 1 = 1	9
+ __1					
1010			0 + 1 = 1	1 + 1 = 0	10
+ __1					
1011				0 + 1 = 1	11
+ __1					
1100		0 + 1 = 1	1 + 1 = 0	1 + 1 = 0	12
+ __1					
1101				0 + 1 = 1	13
+ __1					
1110			0 + 1 = 1	1 + 1 = 0	14
+ __1					
1111				0 + 1 = 1	15

Figure 1.3   Binary counting table.

(a) 1001	(b) 1110	(c) 1010	(d) 0011
+ 0011	+ 1000	+ 0111	+ 0111
1100	10110	10001	1010

1.3.2 Binary Subtraction

The only trick to binary subtraction is understanding how much a borrow actually represents. The easiest way to understand the concept of a borrow is to examine a subtraction example in our native decimal system.

$$
\begin{array}{r}
54 \\
- 8 \\
\hline
46
\end{array}
$$

We cannot subtract 8 from 4, so a borrow is required. Remembering that the second column of a decimal number has a place value of 10, we subtract 1 from 5 (leaving 4) and add the borrow of 10 to 4. Eight subtracted from 14 (10 + 4) is equal to 6 and 0 subtracted from 4 is equal to 4. Now consider an indirect, or double, borrow.

$$
\begin{array}{r}
504 \\
- 8 \\
\hline
496
\end{array}
$$

This time 100 must be borrowed from the third column and added to the value in the second column, yielding a result of 100. Then 10 is borrowed from 100, leaving 90 in the second column and 14 in the first column. Eight from 14 equals 6, 0 from 9 equals 9; and 0 from 4 equals 4. As trivial as the preceding two subtraction examples with borrowing may seem, they are, nonetheless, important illustrations of the actual mechanics of the simple and complex borrow. Now consider the following simple binary subtraction:

$$
\begin{array}{rr}
10 & 1\emptyset^{1+1} \\
- 1 & - 1 \\
\hline
1 & 1
\end{array}
$$

The 1 from the second column is borrowed. Notice that this results in 1 + 1 in the first column (1 + 1 = 10). Test your understanding of binary subtraction with the following examples.

No borrow required:

$$
\begin{array}{r}
1101 \\
- 100 \\
\hline
1001
\end{array}
$$

Elementary borrows:

$$
\begin{array}{rrrr}
1010 & 1101 & 1000 & 1110 \\
- 1 & - 11 & - 100 & - 1101 \\
\hline
1001 & 1010 & 0100 & 0001
\end{array}
$$

Complex borrow:

$$\begin{array}{r} 1100 \\ -\quad\;\; 1 \\ \hline 1011 \end{array}$$

1.4 TTL LOGIC LEVELS AND GATES

The Greek philosophers developed the "study of reason," which is known today as "logic." In the field of logic, arguments containing true and false statements are evaluated for validity. Because digital circuits are capable of only two discrete voltage levels they are called *logic circuits.* The high and low levels of digital circuits can be equated with the concepts of true and false, logic 1 and logic 0, yes and no, or on and off. Some digital circuits equate a high voltage level to true and a low voltage level to false. Other digital circuits work in an opposite manner, equating a low voltage level to true and a high voltage level to false.

Transistor-to-transistor logic (TTL) is one of the oldest and most popular digital *integrated circuit* (IC) families. TTL circuits operate with a power supply of $+5$ V. In an ideal situation $+5$ V on the output of a TTL circuit is interpreted as a *logic* 1 level, and 0 V on the output of a TTL circuit is interpreted as a *logic* 0 level. The actual specifications defining logic levels in TTL circuits must take into account the *loading effects* induced on the output of a TTL circuit by the other circuits that it is driving. Any voltage between $+5$ V and 2 V is considered a logic 1; a voltage between 0 V and 0.8 V is considered a logic 0; a voltage that falls between 0.8 V and 2 V is considered an indeterminate level and usually indicates a circuit malfunction.

The simplest TTL devices are called *logic gates.* A logic gate performs a simple *logic operation* on one or more inputs. Examples of logic functions that we commonly use in conversational English are *AND, OR,* and *NOT.*

Each logic function can be viewed from a *positive-logic* and a *negative-logic* point of view. Figure 1.4 illustrates the schematic symbol and operation of the positive-logic AND gate. If input (a) is high AND input (b) is high, then the output will be high; otherwise, the output will be low.

Figure 1.5 illustrates the schematic symbol and operation of the negative-logic AND gate. If input (a) is low and the OR input (b) is low, then the output will be low; otherwise, the output will be high.

It is important to notice that Figures 1.4 and 1.5 say exactly the same thing but from two different points of view. Figure 1.6 is a summary of the AND function.

Figure 1.7 illustrates the schematic symbol and operation of the positive-logic OR gate. If input (a) is high and the OR input (b) is high, then the output will be high; otherwise, the output will be low.

Figure 1.8 illustrates the schematic symbol and operation of the negative-logic OR gate. If input (a) is low and the AND input (b) is low, then the output will be low; otherwise, the output will be high.

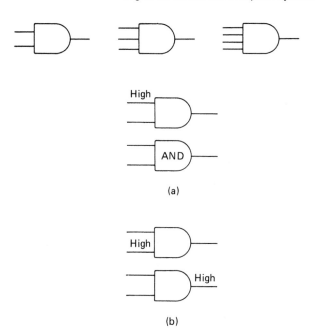

(a)

(b)

Figure 1.4 Positive-logic AND function.

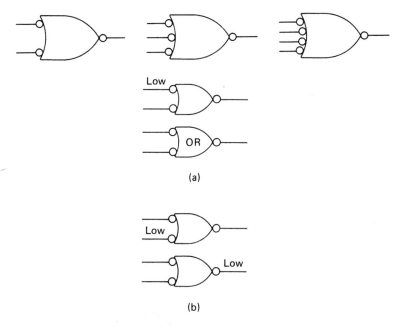

(a)

(b)

Figure 1.5 Negative-logic AND function.

B	A	Out
0	0	0
0	1	0
1	0	0
1	1	1

Figure 1.6 Summary of the AND function.

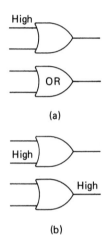

(a)

(b)

Figure 1.7 Positive-logic OR function.

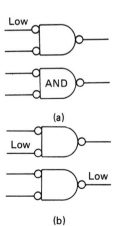

(a)

(b)

Figure 1.8 Negative-logic OR gate.

Once again, notice that both versions of the OR functions say the same thing, but they do so from distinctly different points of view. Figure 1.9 summarizes the OR function.

The third elementary logic function is the simplest because it has only one input. Figure 1.10 illustrates the NOT function as performed by a logic gate called the *inverter*. The inverter simply outputs the logic level that is opposite to the logic level input, thus performing the NOT function.

Figure 1.11 summarizes the difference between the outputs of analog and digital circuits. As one moves the wiper arm of the variable resistor in Figure 1.11(a), the voltage increases or decreases in a continuous and linear fashion. The box in Figure 1.11(b) symbolizes a digital device with three outputs. Unlike the analog circuit, whose output changes in a continuous manner, the output of the digital device "jumps" in discrete steps from count to count.

B	A	Out
0	0	0
0	1	1
1	0	1
1	1	1

Figure 1.9 Summary of the OR function.

(a)   (b)

Input	Output
0	1
1	0

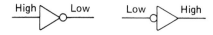

Figure 1.10 The NOT function and the inverter.

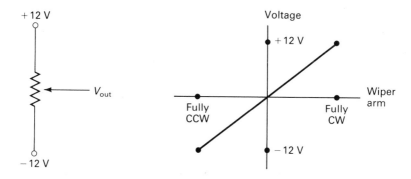

(a) Voltage graphed against wiper arm position

		B_2	B_1	B_0
	0	0	0	0
	1	0	0	1
	2	0	1	0
	3	0	1	1
	4	1	0	0
	5	1	0	1
	6	1	1	0
	7	1	1	1

(b) Output states of A 3-bit digital circuit

Figure 1.11   Outputs of analog and digital circuits.

1.5 THE ELEMENTS OF A COMPUTER SYSTEM

The traditional block diagram of a computer appears in Figure 1.12.

The *central processing unit* (CPU) is the brains of the computer system. In *mainframe* computers the CPU is constructed from many printed circuit boards. In microcomputers, the CPU is implemented in a single IC called a *microprocessor*. A microprocessor is essentially a "CPU on a chip." The CPU executes instructions,

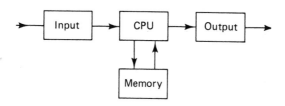

Figure 1.12   Block diagram of a computer.

stores and retrieves data, performs mathematical and logic functions, and controls and monitors the computer system.

Although a CPU can "think," it is deaf and mute and has no memory, which is the reason for the additional four blocks in Figure 1.12. The memory block contains read/write memory (RAM), read-only memory (ROM), and mass storage devices such as floppy and hard disk drives and magnetic tape devices.

Input devices are the "ears" of the computer and allow information from the outside world to pass into the CPU for manipulation and storage. The most familiar input device is the keyboard, which evolved directly from the typewriter keyboard. Other common input devices are the mouse (a cursor pointing device), graphics tablets, digitizers, light pens, bar-code readers, and data acquisition systems.

Output devices are the "voices" of the computer and allow information from the internal world of the computer to pass to the outside world. The most popular output devices are the video display and the printer.

Input and output devices are classified as *peripheral equipment* because they exist outside of the computer system. With the hundreds of different computers and *input/output* (I/O) devices available, how do we know that a particular computer will be compatible with a particular I/O device? The answer to that question is the *standard interface circuit*. I/O devices are never directly connected to computers; instead a circuit called an *I/O port* is employed.

Figure 1.13 illustrates a computer and printer that are interfaced via an I/O port. The job of an I/O port is quite simple. On the peripheral device's side of the interface, the I/O port must conform to an established and widely accepted standard. The computer's side of the I/O port conforms to the individually designed circuitry that is unique to every make and model of computer.

Manufacturers of I/O devices want to appeal to the widest possible market, and all computer manufacturers want their customers to have the greatest selection of peripherals. For this to be possible, manufacturers of peripherals design their products to meet an accepted communications interface standard; computer manufacturers provide I/O ports that also conform to accepted standards. In this way any peripheral device can be connected to any computer, provided that they both support the same interface standard.

The preceding paragraph would be true in an ideal world. Unfortunately, any standard—however followed in good faith—is open to individual interpretation and customization. It is the singular task of this book to overcome these modifications

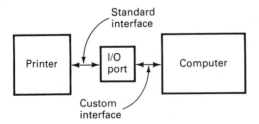

Custom
interface

Figure 1.13 Block diagram of computer/ printer interface.

and deviations to provide the highest level of compatibility between computers and peripherals.

1.6 PARALLEL AND SERIAL INTERFACES

Section 1.3 mentioned that a byte of digital information can represent a letter, numeral, punctuation mark, or standard symbol. I/O ports are designed either to transfer the byte of data on a bit-by-bit basis in a *serial stream* or simply to send the byte in a single *parallel* operation employing eight lines—one for each bit of data.

The model of the *serial interface* in Figure 1.14(b) is constructed from two digital devices called *shift registers*. The *parallel-in–serial-out* (PISO) shift register serializes a byte of data into a single stream of bits. On each rising edge of the clock, the next data bit is transmitted. The *serial-in–parallel-out* (SIPO) shift register provides the complementary function of the PISO shift register. On each falling edge of the clock, the data bit on the serial input is transferred into a storage cell. After eight clock pulses, the byte residing on the inputs of the PISO shift register is also stored on the outputs of the SIPO shift register.

Notice that the data in the serial interface is sent on a single line. Contrast that with the model of the parallel interface illustrated in Figure 1.14(c). Each bit of data is sent on a separate conductor.

The inherent attraction of the serial interface is that it takes only a single conductor to provide communications between devices. A pair of wires can be used so two devices can simultaneously transmit and receive data. The significance of communications via a stream of data bits is that standard two-wire phone circuits can be used to carry on a two-way conversation between a computer and a peripheral. It is this simple feature that is responsible for the popularity of the serial interface. For two devices to carry on a conversation on a parallel interface, at least 16 wires would be required.

The beauty of the parallel interface is its sheer simplicity. A byte of data is placed on the output of the transmitter and a single clock pulse transfers the data in the outputs of the receiver. The serial stream method of exchanging data lends itself to many complexities. For simplification, a clock line is illustrated in Figure 1.14(b). In actual operation a discrete clock is not used. Major considerations are:

How fast is the data stream transmitted?

How many data bits will actually be sent to represent each character?

How will the receiver sense that transmission of a new character has started?

How will the receiver know when the transmission is complete?

How will transmission errors be detected?

How will the receiver indicate to the transmitter that it is ready to receive data?

How will the transmitter indicate to the receiver that it is ready to send data?

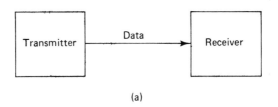

(a)

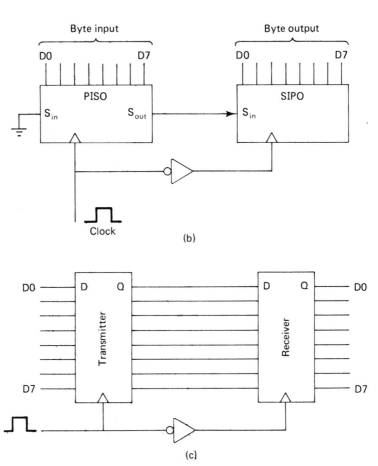

(b)

(c)

Figure 1.14 Serial and parallel interfaces.

How will the receiver indicate to the transmitter that it must temporarily stop sending data and allow it time to process what has already been sent?

These eight points indicate the inherent complexity of serial data communications. We will discover the answers to these questions in Chapters 2 and 3.

These important concepts summarize the material in Chapter 1:

- In analog circuits a number can be represented by a particular voltage level. Noise, lack of precision, and the inability to represent a large range of numbers are insurmountable problems encountered while trying to describe quantities in analog circuits.
- In digital circuits there are only two voltage levels. A square wave is an example of a digital signal.
- Because a square wave has two "fingers," ditigal circuits are best described by the binary number system.
- A bit is a binary digit.
- A group of 8 bits is called a byte. One byte can represent 256 unique numbers or characters.
- A group of 4 bits is called a nibble.
- Digital circuits are called logic circuits because each voltage level can be attributed to true or false, logic 1 or logic 0, yes or no, or on or off.
- In TTL circuits +5 V is called a logic 1 level and 0 V is called a logic 0 level.
- A logic gate is a digital circuit that performs a simple logic operation such as AND, OR, or NOT.
- The block diagram of a computer consists of a CPU, memory, and input/ output ports.
- A microprocessor is a CPU on a chip.
- Peripheral devices are connected to computer systems via input and output ports.
- A standard interface circuit enables manufacturers to design peripheral equipment to be compatible with many different types of computers.
- Serial interfaces communicate via a stream of bits of data and require a minimum of two lines for two-way communications.
- Parallel interfaces send a complete byte of data in one simple operation but require a minimum of 16 lines for two-way communications.
- Serial communication is inherently more complicated than parallel communication because of the characteristics of the bit stream.

2

The ASCII Code

2.1 THE HEXADECIMAL NUMBER SYSTEM

As you discovered in the last chapter, a group of 8 bits (called a byte) is the most common form of digital data. But, eight 1s and 0s side by side tend to blur together and quickly become unreadable. A number system that can be used as a shorthand method to represent a byte is required; yet it must be a close relative of binary, making conversions between itself and base 2 a simple task. The *hexadecimal* number system best suits this purpose. *Hexadecimal* is a combination of the Greek words for 6 (hex) and 10 (decimal); thus hexadecimal is a base-16 number system. The 16 unique symbols in hexadecimal are:

$$0, 1, 2, 3, 4, 5, 6, 7, 8, 9, A, B, C, D, E, F$$

Conveniently, the first 10 symbols are borrowed from our decimal system. The last six symbols are the first letters of the alphabet. (Although the author prefers uppercase, both upper- and lowercase letters are commonly used to represent the last six hex digits.) To determine how many binary bits can be symbolized by one hex digit, recall that four bits define 16 unique combinations; each of these can be symbolized by one hex digit.

Nibble	Hex Digit
0000	0
0001	1
0010	2
0011	3
0100	4
0101	5
0110	6
0111	7
1000	8
1001	9
1010	A
1011	B
1100	C
1101	D
1110	E
1111	F

Conversion between binary and hexademical is simple. Starting with the least significant bit, form nibbles (4 bits). If the last group is less than 4 bits, pad the leading bits with zeros. Each nibble is then assigned a hex digit.

110 1101	11 1010 1110	111 0010	1011 1010
6 D	3 A E	7 2	B A

To convert from hexadecimal to binary, replace each hex digit with its equivalent 4 bits. We will soon discover that hexademimal notation is quite useful for handling digital codes. Hexadecimal numbers are often followed by the letter H to distinguish them from decimal quantities (i.e., 72H.)

2.2 STANDARD DIGITAL CODES

In the English language there are 96 common symbols that represent

Lower- and uppercase letters of the alphabet (a, b, c, . . . A, B, C, . . .)
Digits (0, 1, 2, . . . , 9)
Punctuation marks (., ?, :, (, . . .)
Arithmetic operators (+ , − , = , . . .)
Unit symbols (%, #, $, @, . . .)

The outputs of a digital circuit can be used to represent these symbols. Each symbol is assigned a unique combination of logic 1s and 0s. Before a computer and a printer can communicate, they must agree on the *digital codes* that are used to represent each symbol. We learned in Chapter 1 that the greatest advantage of a standard I/O interface is that it ensures compatibility between computers and peripherals. The same idea can be applied to digital codes. The implementation of a standard digital code guarantees that computers and peripherals will recognize each other's digital representation of a common character set.

Although there are many standard codes employed in the computer industry, the American Standard Code for Information Interchange (ASCII) is the most popular and widely recognized. ASCII is a 7-bit code in which 2^7 (128) characters are represented.

Before we examine ASCII let's take a moment to think about the keys on a typewriter. Most of the keys cause a symbol to be printed by striking an embossed hammer against an ink ribbon and paper. However there are many keys on a typewriter that cause an action to occur instead of printing a character. The return key causes the paper carriage to return to the first column of the left margin and also feeds the paper forward by one line. The backspace key moves the carriage back by one character. The tab key moves the carriage from its present position to the next tab stop. These are examples of *control keys*; keys that cause an action to occur rather than a character to be printed.

2.3 THE ASCII CODE

Figure 2.1 illustrates the ASCII table. Figure 2.1 is a rectangular matrix of 16 rows by 8 columns depicting a total of 128 unique elements. ASCII is a 7-bit code representing 32 control characters and 96 printable characters. Each row and column is labeled in both hexadecimal and binary. This is a great convenience, which you will appreciate when we investigate bit streams.

The 96 standard printable characters illustrated in Figure 2.1 are generated by pressing the appropriate key or the appropriate key while holding down the shift key. Computer keyboards have all the keys of a conventional typewriter and also several special keys. A key labeled Ctrl is the *control key*. The 32 control codes in Figure 2.1 are created by holding down the control key while pressing another key. The control codes in column 0 are generated by holding down the control key and pressing the appropriate key in column 4. Holding down Ctrl and pressing @ generates the code for an ASCII NUL. The standard notation for that control sequence is ˄@, where the ˄ stands for the control key. Thus ˄G generates the code for an ASCII BEL and ˄N generates the code for an ASCII SO. In a similar manner, the control codes for the second column are generated by holding down the Ctrl key and pressing the appropriate key in column 5. A ˄S generates the ASCII code for a DC3, and ˄Q generates an ASCII DC1.

The control codes are further broken into four groups: format effectors, communications controls, information separators, and miscellaneous. We will first examine the format effectors, which provide analogous functions to the control keys of a conventional typewriter.

			Bit 7	0	0	0	0	1	1	1	1
			Bit 6	0	0	1	1	0	0	1	1
			Bit 5	0	1	0	1	0	1	0	1
Bit 4	Bit 3	Bit 2	Bit 1	Col. / Row	0	1	2	3	4	5	6	7
0	0	0	0	0	NUL	DLE	SP	0	@	P	`	p
0	0	0	1	1	SOH	DC1	!	1	A	Q	a	q
0	0	1	0	2	STX	DC2	"	2	B	R	b	r
0	0	1	1	3	ETX	DC3	#	3	C	S	c	s
0	1	0	0	4	EOT	DC4	$	4	D	T	d	t
0	1	0	1	5	ENQ	NAK	%	5	E	U	e	u
0	1	1	0	6	ACK	SYN	&	6	F	V	f	v
0	1	1	1	7	BEL	ETB	'	7	G	W	g	w
1	0	0	0	8	BS	CAN	(	8	H	X	h	x
1	0	0	1	9	HT	EM	)	9	I	Y	i	y
1	0	1	0	A	LF	SUB	*	:	J	Z	j	z
1	0	1	1	B	VT	ESC	+	;	K	[	k	{
1	1	0	0	C	FF	FS	,	<	L	\	l	|
1	1	0	1	D	CR	GS	-	=	M	]	m	}
1	1	1	0	E	SO	RS	.	>	N	^	n	~
1	1	1	1	F	SI	US	/	?	O	_	o	DEL

Figure 2.1 The ASCII code.

2.3.1 Format Effectors

BS (backspace) 08H: ^H. The BS character causes the cursor on a video display or the print head to move back one space. A backspace can be described as either *destructive* or *nondestructive*. A destructive backspace moves the cursor back one space and also erases the character under its final position. Typewriters use a nondestructive backspace; the carriage is simply moved back one position. Printers must use a nondestructive backspace, and video displays use both types of backspaces.

HT (horizontal tab) 09H: ^I. The HT character is equivalent to the tab key on a typewriter. On receiving an HT character, the cursor or print head will move to the next tab position. Tab positions on video displays and printers, just like tab positions on typewriters, are programmable. When applications programs, such as word processors or program editors, are invoked, a *default set* of tab positions is used. Most applications allow the user to redefine (reprogram) the tab positions. It is the responsibility of the program to calculate the next tab position when it receives an HT character from the keyboard. Computer keyboards have a tab key, which usually generates the same code as ^I.

You should exercise caution with tabs on printers. In an initialized (power-up) state many printers do not have a set of default tab positions and will consequently ignore HT characters. A sequence of special characters must be sent to the printer to program the tab positions prior to normal printing operations. We will discuss the concepts of *printer-driver* programs in Chapter 5.

LF (line feed) 0AH: ^J.
CR (carriage return) 0DH: ^M. When the return key on a typewriter is pressed, two actions occur. The carriage returns to the first print column and the paper is advanced to the next line. On the video display of a computer or terminal, CR returns the cursor to the first column of the present line, and LF moves the cursor down by one line or the paper up by one line (thus the term *line feed*.) The column in which the cursor or print head is residing prior to the receipt of the LF is not changed. The action of a typewriter return key is a combination of the characters CR and LF. Breaking a traditional typewriter return into two distinct actions results in a greater flexibility for output to video displays and printers. A *newline character* is defined as sending a CR/LF sequence.

Commands are usually terminated by a CR. For example, to get a listing of the programs and files on a floppy disk, one might type in the command dir <CR>, where <CR> indicates that the execution of the command begins after the CR key is pressed. (The CR key is also called the "enter" key.)

Printers usually wait to receive a complete line of characters before starting the printing process. A CR indicates to a printer that it has been sent all the characters in the line and can proceed with printing.

FF (form feed) 0CH: ^ **L.**   The FF character has distinctly different meanings if sent to a printer or a video display. Printer paper comes in the form of continuous sheets (bordered by pin feed holes) that are folded into pages and placed into a cardboard box. Each page is called a *form*. The form-feed character instructs the printer to execute the appropriate number of line feeds to bring the beginning of the next form in line with the print head. This operation implies that printers must know the number of lines per form and decrement the line count each time a LF character is received. In Chapter 7 we investigate the typical indicators and switch settings on printers.

When sent to a video display, ^ L causes the cursor to move one space to the right in complementary fashion to a backspace.

VT (vertical tab) 0BH: ^ **K.**   VT also has different meanings to a printer and a video display. When sent to a printer, ^ K provides a similar function to the HT character. A VT character causes a printer to line feed to the next programmed verticle tab position.

When sent to a video display, ^ K causes the cursor to move up one line. This is the complementary operation to a line feed.

Most computer keyboards have four keys labeled with arrows: up, down, left, and right. These *cursor-control* keys are used to move the cursor to any position on the display. Early computer keyboards did not have cursor-control keys. Instead ^ H, ^ J, ^ L, and ^ K key sequences were used to move the cursor around the screen.

	Control Keys
Cursor left	^ H
Cursor down	^ J
Cursor up	^ K
Cursor right	^ L

2.3.2 Communication-Control Characters

The communication-control characters are

SOH (start of header)

STX (start of text)

ETX (end of text)

EOT (end of transmission)

ENQ (inquiry)

ACK (acknowledge)

DLE (data link escape)

NAK (negative acknowledge)

SYN (synchronous idle)

ETB (end of block)

These control characters are used during complex synchronous communication and data-transfer protocols. The study of these topics is not relevant to the material in this book. Exceptions to this are the EXT (03H), EOT (04H), and SUB (1AH) characters. People who use microcomputers and understand the basic concepts of an *operating system* should know the meaning of these characters.

The EXT character is generated with ˆ C. On most computers typing ˆ C *interrupts* the currently executing program and returns the user to the command level of the operating system.

EOT (ˆ D) is used by the UNIX operating system, typically to indicate that the user has completed input and the program should continue execution. This is called an *end-of-file* (EOF) character.

SUB (ˆ Z) is used by the popular CPM/80 and PC-DOS microcomputer operating systems as the last byte in a data file. When a program running under PC-DOS reads the byte 1AH, it knows that the end of file has been reached.

2.3.3 Information-Separator Codes

The information-separator codes are:

FS (file separator)
GS (group separator)
RS (record separator)
US (unit separator)

As with the communications control characters, in this book we have no general interest in the information-separator codes.

2.3.4 Miscellaneous Codes

Many of the characters in the miscellaneous group have universally accepted meanings. We examine the most important of these control characters.

NUL (null) 00H: ˆ @.   NUL is often used to pad the beginning of a transmission of characters. This is required in situations where a receiving device (most often a printer) appears to miss the first few characters in a message. NUL is also used as a termination character when programming video displays and printers.

BEL (bell) 07H: ˆ G.   When a video display receives a BEL character, it generates a tone. BEL is used to gain a user's attention to indicate an illegal entry or any other important event.

DC1–DC4 (device control): ˆ Q–ˆ T.   These four codes are used to control the operation of video displays and printers. Of special interest are DC1 (ˆ Q) and DC3 (ˆ S). DC1 called *X-ON* and DC3 is called *X-OFF*, where X is an abbreviation for transmission. Consider the typical situation where the computer is sending information so quickly that it is scrolling off the top of the video display before it can be read. An ˆ S (X-OFF) sent to the computer causes it to stop sending data to the video display; a ˆ Q (X-ON) indicates that the computer can resume data transmission. This use of X-ON and X-OFF is called *flow control* or *software handshaking*.

Although X-ON is the most correct and formal way to indicate that the data transmission may resume, in general practice the first key depressed following X-OFF restarts the data transmission.

The most popular use of flow control is to reconcile the differing speeds of computers and printers. Because computers are electronic devices, they process data at an extremely fast rate. Printers, on the other hand, are electro-mechanical and are thousands of times slower than the computers from which they receive data. How can we be sure that the computer is not sending data so quickly that the printer is overrun and loses or garbles characters? All printers have a small amount of *buffer memory*. When the buffer is almost full, the printer transmits X-OFF to the computer. The computer reacts by suspending the data transmission and patiently waits to receive an X-ON character from the printer before it resumes sending data. In this manner a lightning-fast computer can converse with an excruciatingly slow printer without suffering loss of data.

Esc (escape) 1BH: ˆ [.   Another key that is unique to computer keyboards is the Esc (escape) key. To exploit all the functions available on video displays and printers, there must be more than the 32 control codes of the ASCII code. The concept of an *escape sequence* is quite simple. When a video display or printer receives an Esc code, it interprets the next one or more printable characters as a command instead of data. This effectively creates an infinite number of unique commands. Modern printers have many features that are programmed or invoked via escape sequences. We learn more about escape sequences in Chapter 5.

Del (delete) 7FH.   There is one special control character that does reside in columns 0 or 1 of Figure 2.1. The Del character is all logic 1s (111 1111). The history of this character goes back to the days of *paper tape*. From the early 1960s through the 1970s, paper tape was used to store digital data. ASCII characters were represented by the presence or lack of holes punched in the tape. No hole represented a logic 0, whereas a hole represented a logic 1. To delete a character, all the holes had to be punched out; thus the code of all logic 1s is used to represent a delete character. Many computer systems and documentation call the Del character by its common alias, *rub-out*. Both Del and rub-out are commonly used to reference ASCII 7FH.

Like other control codes that we have examined, Del has many uses. On a video display it is used to delete the character that is presently residing under the cursor. (This should not be confused with the BS, which moves the cursor one space to the left and then possibly deletes that character.)

The other use of Del cannot be fully understood at this time. It is used as a *sync character* to synchronize a receiver to a bit stream. We will examine that issue in Chapter 8.

2.4 PRINTABLE ASCII CHARACTERS

The remaining 95 characters (96 minus Del) represent letters, numerals, punctuation marks, arithmetic operators, and unit symbols that can be represented on a video display or printer. The codes for these characters were not selected at random. ASCII is a well-thought-out and practical code that enables programs to do common translations of letters and numerals.

ASCII 20H is the space. A space should not be mistaken for a NUL. When a computer or terminal is turned-on, the display memory is initialized to ASCII 20H. The display is actually exhibiting 24 lines by 80 columns of the ASCII space character. ASCII 20H is used to provide spaces between characters and blank lines on video displays.

2.4.1 Digits and Letters

Consider column 3 of the ASCII table, which contains the digits 0–9. Notice that the least significant nibbles of the codes representing the decimal digits are the binary representations of the digits themselves. To determine whether a certain character is a decimal digit, its code can be tested to see if it falls between 30H and 39H. If the bits in the most significant nibble are reset to logic 0s, the actual value of the digit is recovered. Also notice that the only difference between the upper- and lowercase letters is the most significant nibble. This makes translation between upper- and lowercase a trivial chore.

Words can be alphabetized by ordering their ASCII codes from the lowest (starting with A at 41H) to the highest (ending with Z at 5AH.) In a program that alphabetizes by ASCII code, a word starting with a capital letter always appears before a word starting with a lowercase letter. In this manner, programs written in BASIC can have a conditional statement in the form of

```
If A$ > B$ then _____
```

The ASCII value of the characters comprising the string variables is being compared in such a statement. Thus A < B and Z < a.

2.4.2 Extended 8-Bit ASCII

You may have wondered why the ASCII code is only 7 bits when the standard size of data is the 8-bit style. Microcomputer manufacturers use the extra bit to form their own proprietary extensions to standard ASCII. These extra 128 characters are special block graphics symbols, foreign language sets, Greek letters, and mathematical or engineering symbols. Beware! Extended ASCII codes are different for every make and model of microcomputer.

These important concepts summarize the material in Chapter 2:

- The hexademical number system is a shorthand means of representing long strings of bits.
- One hexadecimal digit can represent one nibble.
- ASCII is a universally accepted 7-bit code representing 32 control codes and 96 printable characters.
- Each ASCII character is usually represented by two hexademical digits.
- Each of the 32 control codes is generated from the keyboard by holding down the Ctrl key while depressing another key, whose code appears in the fourth or fifth column of the ASCII table.
- The combination of the CR and LF characters is called a new-line character and is used to emulate a typewriter carriage return.
- A sheet of computer page is called a form. An FF character advances the paper in a printer to the first line of the next form.
- Control codes can be used to move the cursor up, down, right, or left.
- The ^ symbol is used to represent the control key. Thus ^C means to hold down the Ctrl key while depressing the C.
- A ^C is used to interrupt a program that is currently executing.
- A ^D is used as an EOF market in Unix, and ^Z is used as an EOF marker in CP/M-80 and MS-DOS.
- The DC1 and DC3 characters are popularly known as X-ON and X-OFF. X-ON/X-OFF flow control is used to reconcile RS-232 devices that send/ receive, or process data at different speeds.
- An escape sequence is defined as the Esc code followed by one or more printable characters. Escape sequences are used to generate an infinite number of commands for programmable peripherals.
- Del is the last character in the ASCII code. It is often used to synchronize the bit stream.
- Extended 8-bit ASCII is used to represent block graphics characters, foreign language sets, Greek letters, and mathematical and engineering symbols. These 128 printable characters are unique to each make and model of computer.

3

RS-232
Interface Standard

In Chapter 1 we established the need for a widely followed and accepted I/O interface standard. The *RS-232 standard* (RS stands for recommended standard) was established by the *EIA* (Electronic Industries Association) in the 1960s to facilitate compatibility and interchangeability between computers and peripheral devices that were connected via serial ports. Most literature refers to RS-232 as RS-232C, which is the latest revision. We will drop the C and simply use RS-232 as the name of the interface standard.

The RS-232 interface has many common equivalents and aliases:

1. **EIA standard:** The EIA has had considerable influence on the creation of the standard.

2. **V.24:** The *CCITT (Consultive Committee International Telegraph and Telephone)* is a United Nations group that recommends international standards. The CCITT's V.24 standard is equivalent to the EIA's RS-232C.

3. *TTY (teletype) port:* Teletypewriters were the first printing computer output devices. For historical reasons, serial ports on mini- and mainframe computers are still often called TTY ports.

RS-232 defines the electrical signal characteristics, mechanical interface, and the functional description of the interchange circuits in a large technical document available from the EIA.

Contact:

EIA Engineering Department
Standard Sales
2001 Eye Street N.W.
Washington DC 20006
(202) 457-4966

In this chapter we examine RS-232 in an intuitive and practical light.

3.1 DATA TERMINAL EQUIPMENT AND DATA COMMUNICATIONS EQUIPMENT

It is easiest to understand the RS-232 connection by describing the application for which it was originally designed. A *computer terminal* is a combination video display and keyboard. Most terminals are connected to computers via an RS-232 serial interface port. Consider the situation where an individual needs to access a computer from a distant location. How can the remote terminal be physically connected to the computer? Wherever we travel throughout the world, the two utilities that are inevitability available are AC power and telephone service.

3.1.1 The modem

Figure 3.1 depicts the connection of a remote terminal and a computer via a standard telephone line. The terminal and computer are not directly connected; they are separated by devices called *modems*. Digital waveforms can not be transmitted

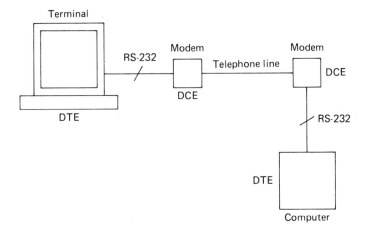

Figure 3.1 Remote terminal/computer connection.

over long lengths of wire. Every wire has an associated amount of capacitance and resistance.

Figure 3.2(a) illustrates the resistance and capacitance as it is distributed along the length of a wire. You may recall the following facts from basic DC theory:

1. Resistances in series are accumulative.
2. Capacitances in parallel are also accumulative.

Figure 3.2(b) indicates that the resistance and capacitance in a wire can be symbolized as having total values of R_T and C_T, respectively. If a square wave is input into the circuit in Figure 3.2(b), it will be distorted on the output, as depicted in Figure 3.2(c). This is because R_T and C_T form a circuit called an *integrator*. It is the basic nature of capacitors to oppose any change in voltage. At the first moment that the input changes to a logic 1 level, the capacitor will appear to be a short cir-

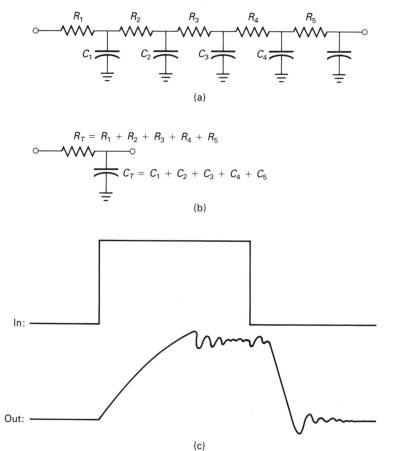

Figure 3.2   The effects of capacitance and resistance of a long wire.

cuit to ground, and the entire input voltage will be dropped across R_T. It will take a total of five RC time constants before V_{out} *is equal to* V_{in}. The output is no longer a digital signal! For an appreciable length of time, it has levels that exist between a logic 0 and a logic 1.

Figure 3.2 leads us to believe that digital communications cannot occur directly between a terminal and a computer employing standard telephone lines. Telephone lines were designed to carry signals in the audible (voice) range of frequencies. The modems in Figure 3.1 are devices that convert the two levels of a digital signal into two different tones. These audible tones can propagate along commercial phone lines with little degradation. The modem is a *transceiver,* which means it transmits and also receives data. The process of impressing a digital signal onto an *analog carrier* frequency is called *modulation.* The reverse process of recovering a digital signal from an analog carrier is called *demodulation.* Thus the term *Mod*ulator-*Dem*odulator is contracted to form *modem.*

3.1.2 Terminal and Communications Equipment

The word *terminal* indicates the end of the line, as in a bus terminal. In the phrase *data terminal equipment* (DTE), terminal indicates the two extreme ends of the data communications circuit. In Figure 3.1 the DTEs are the terminal and the computer. The modems are defined as *data communications equipment* (DCEs), because they exist to provide communications capability between two DTEs. (Although they are less frequently used, other terms attributed to the initials DCE are *data circuit terminating equipment* and *data channel equipment.*)

The terminal-modem and computer-modem connections conform to the RS-232 standard, whereas the connection between the two modems is a standard two-wire phone line. The DTE and DCE each have specific responsibilities in the RS-232 communications scheme.

3.2 THE RS-232 CONNECTOR PINOUT

Before we examine the pinout of the RS-232 connector, we need to consider an important term. Remember that a digital signal is either at a high or low level. On the control lines of the RS-232 interface, a high level means ''on'' and a low level means ''off.'' The phrase ''the control line is asserted'' means that the digital level on a particular control line was taken from a low level to a high level. The phraseology ''to assert'' will be employed throughout this book.

Figure 3.3 illustrates the RS-232 connector. All 25 pins are explicitly defined in RS-232. Figure 3.4 defines the 9 pins that are usually employed in asynchronous communications.

Let's examine the meaning of each of these pins as they are employed in a terminal-modem or computer-modem connection. The RS-232 pins that we will study can be divided into three groups: grounds, data, and handshaking.

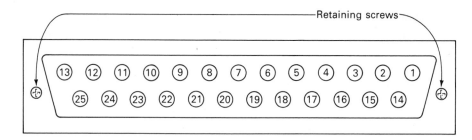

Figure 3.3   RS-232 "D-type" connector—front view.

Pin	Name	Abbreviation
1	Frame ground	FG
2	Transmit data	TD
3	Receive data	RD
4	Request to send	RTS
5	Clear to send	CTS
6	Data set ready	DSR
7	Signal ground	SG
8	Data carrier detect	DCD
20	Data terminal ready	DTR

Figure 3.4   Most popular pins implemented in RS-232 connections.

3.2.1. Grounds

Frame ground: FG (pin 1).   The *frame ground* (FG) is often left unconnected. When it is used, FG is connected to the frame of the terminal or modem or to earth ground. A proper FG guarantees that no dangerous voltages exist on the case of terminals or modems. For that reason, FG is also called *protective ground*. FG also helps cancel noise that can be induced on the frame of equipment if it is not at earth-ground potential.

Signal ground: SG (pin 7). All signals in the RS-232 interface are referenced to the *signal ground* (SG). This ground must be present and continuous for proper circuit operation.

3.2.2. Data

Transmit data: TD (pin 2). Direction: DTE → DCE. Data travels from the DTE (terminal or computer) to the modem via pin 2, TD.

Receive data: RD (pin 3). Direction: DTE ← DCE. Data travels from the DCE (modem) to the DTE via pin 3, RD. It is important to note that the RS-232 transmit and receive data pins are defined from the DTE's point of view. Thus the DCE receives data on pin 2 (TD) and transmits data on pin 3 (RD).

Handshaking. *Handshaking* describes the cooperation between devices that are communicating or exchanging data. Each device must indicate the status of its transmitter and receiver. In the last chapter we examined the flow control *(software handshaking)* characters X-ON and X-OFF. In this section we examine the *hardware handshaking* pins of the RS-232 interface.

Request to send: RTS (pin 4). Direction: DTE → DCE. *Request to send* (RTS) is taken to an active level to indicate that the DTE is ready to transmit data. The DCE's usual response is to activate its carrier and prepare to translate the digital signals from the DTE into the appropriate analog signals.

Clear to send: CTS (pin 5). Direction: DTE ← DCE. So that the DTE knows that the modem has enabled its carrier and that data transmission can commence, the DCE brings *clear to send* (CTS) to an active level. This is the central idea behind the concept of handshaking: One device indicates status and the other device responds in turn.

Consider the sequence: the DTE asserts RTS and, after a slight delay, the DCE responds with an active level on CTS. Until CTS goes active, the DTE will not enable its transmitter.

Data terminal ready: DTR (pin 20). Direction: DTE → DCE. *Data terminal ready* (DTR) is asserted by the DTE when it is powered up and ready. An active level on DTR indicates to the DCE that it is connected to a "live" DTE.

Data set ready: DSR (pin 6). Direction: DTE ← DCE. "Data set" is an older term for a data communications device. For the sake of this discussion, data set and modem are equivalent. Data set ready (DSR) is the DCE's equivalent to DTR. When DSR is asserted, the DTE is informed that it is connected to a "live" DCE.

Let's think about the process that occurs when a terminal and modem are used to form a remote connection with a modem and a computer, as illustrated in Figure 3.1.

1. Each device is powered up and ready, and their respective device-alive signals are asserted (DTR for the terminal and DSR for the modem).
2. The terminal wants to send data, so it asserts RTS.
3. The modem activates the analog carrier (also known as "raising its carrier") and asserts CTS.
4. The user or modem dials the phone number of the remote modem and waits for an answer.

Pin 8 is used so that the terminal knows when it is finally connected to the remote computer and can consequently start sending data. Pin 8 on the RS-232 connector is called *data carrier detect* (DCD), formally known in the RS-232 specification as *received line signal detect* (RLSD). When the local modem senses the carrier of a remote modem over the phone line, it knows that the connection has been accomplished and asserts DCD. A high level on DCD tells the terminal that it is connected to a remote device and data communication can commence.

Data carrier detect: DCD (pin 8). Direction: DTE ← DCE. DCD informs the DTE that a remote connection has been made. Some documents refer to DCD by its formal name of RLSD; yet others abbreviate DCD to CD (carrier detect).

3.3 RS-232 VOLTAGE LEVELS

The following table indicates RS-232 voltage levels and their standard interpretations.

Voltage	Logic	Control	Teletype Terminology
+3 V to +25 V	0	On	Space
−3 V to −25 V	1	Off	Mark

In contrast to TTL logic levels, where the more positive voltage is a logic 1 and the more negative voltage is a logic 0, RS-232 employs *negative-logic levels;* the more positive voltage in the circuit (+3 V to +25 V) is a logic 0, and the more negative voltage (−3 V to −25 V) is a logic 1. A voltage that falls between +3 V and −3 V is an indeterminate level as is a TTL voltage that falls between 0.8 V and 2.0 V.

The two most popular designations describing RS-232 line levels are inherited from teletype terminology. A line at a logic 1 level is said to be a *mark*. A person who is described as "marking time" is said to be in an idle or unproductive state.

An RS-232 device that is not sending data holds its transmit line at a *marking level*—a logic 1. The equivalent teletype term for a logic 0 is a *space*. A data line that is at a *spacing level* is actively transmitting a logic 0. We will learn more about the actual data stream in Chapter 4.

It is natural to think of data lines as carrying logic 1 and logic 0 levels. However, the control lines that perform hardware handshaking are more precisely described as being *on* or *off*. The words *on, active, and asserted* are used to describe a handshaking line at a logic 0 level. The words *off, inactive, or disasserted* are used to describe a handshaking line that is at a logic 1 level. The important idea is that when a control line is a logic 1, it is in a marking or idling state. When a control line is asserted to a logic 0 level, it is in an active, or on, state.

When we state that a terminal will bring RTS to an active level to indicate its intention to send data, that means the line will experience a voltage transition from an inactive level (-3 V to -25 V) to an active level ($+3$ V to $+25$ V).

Most RS-232 devices operate with $+12$ V and -12 V power supplies. A typical mark is from -9 V to -12 V and a typical space is from $+9$ V to $+12$ V. Voltages out of this range usually indicate a circuit or interface malfunction.

3.4 A FIRST APPROXIMATION ANALYSIS OF THE INTERFACE

Figure 3.5 depicts an extremely simplified model of an RS-232 transmitter, transmission line, and RS-232 receiver.

The transmitter is commonly called a *driver* and the receiver is called the *terminator* because it is at the end of the circuit and acts as a load for the transmitter. Let's examine each element in the model.

V_{out}: driver open circuit output voltage. The value V_{out} is the mark or space output from the transmitter under an ideal no-load condition. This level is equal to the positive or negative voltages used to power the RS-232 driver IC.

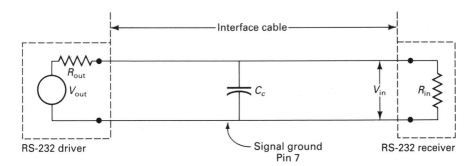

Figure 3.5   Electrical model of a communications interface.

R$_{out}$: driver output resistance.   In an ideal circuit, R_{out} is equal to 0 Ω. In practical circuits all drivers have a measurable amount of output resistance. As the current load on a driver increases, its effective output voltage is decreased by the amount of the current times the value of R_{out}, as indicated by Ohm's law:

$$V_{out \ (actual)} = V_{out \ (internal)} - (I_{out} \times R_{out})$$

Suppose that the output of an RS-232 driver is shorted to signal ground or the opposite logic level of another RS-232 output. (Space to mark or mark to space.) The RS-232 specification guarantees that R_{out} will be of sufficient value to safely limit the short-circuit output current and protect the internal circuitry of the driver.

Important note.   Almost all manufacturers of RS-232 peripherals and computer systems indicate that the output of RS-232 drivers should not be shorted to ground or to the output of other drivers because of the possibility of circuit destruction. This disclaimer is used to limit the manufacturer's liability. Although it has been the experience of the author that any RS-232 driver can be shorted to ground or shorted to the outputs of other drivers without inducing circuit failures, this practice is performed at the user's risk.

C$_c$: Transmission cable capacitance.   As indicated in Figure 3.2, line capacitance has a disastrous effect on the wave shape of digital signals. The value of C_c, the transmission cable capacitance, is the major factor that will limit the practical length of the RS-232 interface cable.

R$_{in}$: Terminator input resistance.   In an ideal situation the terminator input resistance is of infinite value, which means that the terminator will not require any input drive current. In a typical RS-232 receiver IC, R_{in} is many times the value of R_{out}. Thus in the voltage divider formed by R_{out} and R_{in}, the majority of the voltage will fall across R_{in} and appears as V_{in} for the receiver. R_{in} must be able to withstand the maximum RS-232 input values of $+25$ and -25 V without sustaining damage to the receiver.

You may have noticed that the output capacitance of the transmitter, the input capacitance of the receiver, and the resistance of the interface cable have been ignored. The effect of these quantities is so slight that they can be safely ignored in a first approximation analysis of the RS-232 circuit.

3.5 NONSTANDARD 9-PIN RS-232 CONNECTORS

Because only 9 of the 25 pins of the RS-232 interface are used for the majority of applications, many computer and peripheral manufacturers have developed 9-pin RS-232 connectors. Figure 3.6 illustrates the RS-232 connector used with the IBM-PC/AT microcomputer. The 9-pin connector is used to save connector space on the

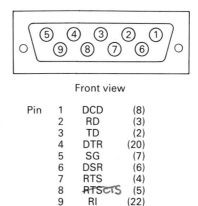

Front view

	Pin	1	DCD	(8)
		2	RD	(3)
		3	TD	(2)
		4	DTR	(20)
		5	SG	(7)
		6	DSR	(6)
		7	RTS	(4)
		8	~~RTS~~CTS	(5)
		9	RI	(22)

Figure 3.6   IBM-PC/AT 9-Pin RS-232
connector.

back panels of computers and peripherals. This connector is *not standard* and differs from manufacturer to manufacturer.

Figure 3.6 shows an RS-232 pin that was not listed in Figure 3.4. Ring indicator (RI) goes to an active level (space) when the modem has received the ring of an incoming call. Although this pin is often not employed, it is still present in most 9-pin RS-232 connectors.

These important concepts summarize the material in Chapter 3:

- The RS-232 standard is also known as the EIA interface or V.24.
- RS-232 ports are often called TTY ports on minicomputers and communications devices.
- Because of the excessive amount of capacitance in wires, digital communications cannot occur directly between geographically distant devices.
- Modem is derived from *mod*ulator/*dem*odulator.
- A modem is a communications device that converts digital pulses into analog signals, which can be transmitted on standard phone lines without degradation.
- DTEs are connected at the ends of a data communications circuit. Terminals, printers, and computers are DTEs.
- DCEs are modems or other devices that are used to facilitate communications between DTEs.
- FG is used to insure that dangerous voltages do not exist between equipment.
- All signals on the RS-232 interface are referenced to SG.
- The TD and RD lines are described from the DTE's point of view.
- Handshaking is the exchange of status between devices that are communicating.
- Handshaking can take place in hardware (via RTS, CTS, DTR, DSR, and DCD) or software (X-ON/X-OFF flow control).

- The term *assert* means to bring to an active level.
- The DTE asserts RTS to indicate that it is ready to transmit data. The DCE responds by raising its carrier and asserting CTS.
- The DTE asserts DTR to indicate that a device is on-line.
- Data Set is another name for a modem.
- The DCE asserts DSR to indicate that a device is on-line.
- DCD (also called RLSD) is used to indicate that the carrier of a remote modem has been sensed by the local modem.
- An RS-232 voltage between +3 V and +25 V is described as a logic 0 level, a control-line on, or a space.
- An RS-232 voltage between −3 V and −25 V is described as a logic 1 level, control-line off, or a mark.
- An RS-232 voltage between +3 V and −3 V is indeterminate and always indicates a circuit malfunction.
- The words *on, active,* and *asserted* are used to describe an RS-232 handshaking line that is at a logic 0 level.
- The words *off, inactive,* and *disasserted* are used to describe an RS-232 handshaking line that is at a logic 1 level.
- Most RS-232 interfaces operate at +12 V and −12 V levels.
- The major factor that limits the length of an RS-232 transmission line is the total amount of capacitance associated with the interface cable.
- Nine-pin RS-232 connectors are becoming popular, but a standard pinout does not yet exist.

4

Structure of the Bit Stream and the UART

In Chapter 3 we learned the characteristics of the RS-232 interface and logic levels. We are now going to examine the actual stream of data bits as they propagate along the serial transmission line. In the second part of this chapter, the programmable serial communications interface controller called the UART and RS-232 driver and receiver ICs are examined.

4.1 SPEED OF THE BIT STREAM

The type of serial communications that we will investigate is called *asynchronous serial communications*. Asynchronous literally means "without regard to time." In asynchronous communications, data comes in irregular bursts, not in a steady or continuous stream. Each data burst is composed of the bits required to form one or more ASCII characters. Some transmitters send each character as it is *serialized;* other transmitters store characters in a buffer and send the burst of data bits in a large block that contains many characters.

There are two important questions that must be answered before we can understand how two devices can communicate on an *asynchronous serial link*. How does the receiver know the following?

1. How fast will the data be sent?
2. When has the transmitter actually started sending data? (Remember that data will be sent in unpredictable bursts.)

The speed at which data is sent along a serial communications line is called the *baud rate*. Baud rate is expressed in units of bits per second. An RS-232 data link communicating at 9600 baud is capable of sending 9600 bits of data and *framing information* in 1 second. (The concept of framing information is studied in the next section.)

You may hear arguments that the terms *baud rate* and *bits per second* are not equivalent. Technically speaking, this is true, but in common usage baud rate and bits per second are considered synonymous.

It is important to understand that the baud rate depicts the maximum possible number of bits per second. Because asynchronous information is sent in bursts, only a small percentage of this *through-put* is actually realized.

How wide is each data bit sent at a speed of 9600 baud? If a maximum of 9600 bits can be sent in 1 second, then the inverse of the baud rate must describe the width of one *bit cell*.

$$\frac{1}{\text{baud rate}} = \text{period of a bit} = \frac{1}{9600} = 104 \ \mu s$$

Assume that the transmitter and receiver both agree that the data will be sent at 9600 baud. The transmitter will send data bits that are 104 μs wide, and the receiver will partition the incoming data stream into individual 104-μs bit cells. Thus, although the data will be sent at irregular (asynchronous) intervals, the width of a particular data bit is a constant that is always equal to the inverse of the baud rate.

4.2 THE START BIT

In Chapter 3 we stated that an inactive transmit data line is held at a marking (logic 1) level. Consider the case when the first data bit sent is a logic 1; the receiver would miss it because the voltage level on the data line would remain at -12 V and the line would appear to remain inactive. How will the receiver know when data transmission has started? The answer to that question is a simple, yet powerful, mechanism that makes asynchronous serial communications possible.

The transmission of each character on an asynchronous communications line is prefaced by a *start bit*. This start bit is a space (logic 0) that has the duration of one bit cell. Consider the reactions of a receiver on a 9600 baud asynchronous line. In an inactive or resting state, the RD input is a mark. The action of the RD as it changes from a mark to a space indicates the presence of a start bit; a stream of data bits will follow in 104-μs cells.

Figure 4.1 illustrates the snapshot of an ASCII "V" (101 0110) as it travels along a serial transmission cable. It is customary to transmit the character out of the parallel-in–serial-out transmit shift register starting with the least significant bit. Let's analyze the events labeled as T_0 through T_9 in Figure 4.1.

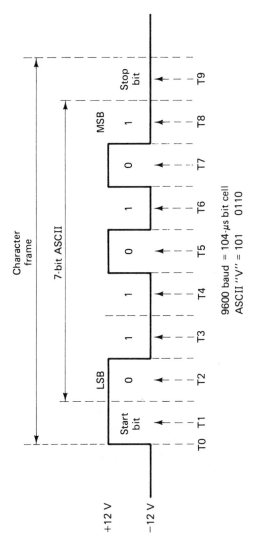

Figure 4.1 ASCII "V" bit stream at RS-232 levels.

9600 baud = 104-μs bit cell
ASCII "V" = 101   0110

T_0: This mark-to-space transition alerts the receiver that the transmission of a
new character has begun.

T_1: The receiver waits a length of time equal to one-half of a bit cell (at 9600
baud, this is 0.52 μs) and then resamples the RD input. If it is still a space,
the receiver is guaranteed that it has sensed a legitimate start bit. If at T_1 the
RD line has returned to a marking level, the false start bit is attributed to a
glitch or a noisy line. The event is disregarded and the receiver waits for the
occurrence of another start bit.

Sampling each bit cell in the center eliminates the leading- and trailing-edge
ringing that is associated with digital signals transmitted on high-capacitance lines.

T_2: The receiver waits for a period of 1 bit cell (0.04 μs) and samples the RD
line to establish the logic level of the least significant bit of the ASCII character.

T_3–T_8: The next 6 bit cells are sampled every 104 μs to obtain the logic values of
the respective bits. After T_8 all 7 data bits have been captured and the
receiving circuitry can reconstruct the parallel byte of "101 0110" into an
ASCII "V".

After the last bit is sent, the transmitter holds TD at a mark for at least 1 bit
cell. This is called the *stop bit*. The stop bit indicates that all the data bits have been
sent and the transmission of the character is complete.

The start and stop bits are like bookends that form the first and last bit of the
character frame. Every character in asynchronous serial communications is enclosed in such a frame. If the receiver counts the start bit and the appropriate number of data bits and then does not sense a marking level, this indicates a *framing
error* and the reception of an invalid character. There are many reasons for the occurrence of framing errors, which are explored in Chapter 8. In Figure 4.1 a total of
9 bits were sent, only 7 of which carried character data. The other 2 bits were used
to frame the asynchronous character. Simple asynchronous serial communications
does not come without a price. The start and stop bits add 28% overhead to the bit
stream. There is a method of implementing serial communications without framing
each character with a start and stop bit. It is called *synchronous serial communications* which will not be examined in this book.

4.3 CHECKING FOR ERRORS IN THE BIT STREAM

Sampling precisely in the center of the bit cell greatly improves the chances that the
logic level of a data bit will be received correctly. Also the presence of the start and
stop bits guarantees that the correct number of data bits have been read; yet serial
transmission errors still occur. The incorrect reading of just one bit can corrupt an
entire file of data. A simply implemented mechanism that can validate the integrity
of each data byte received is needed to guarantee error-free communications.

When two objects are equal they are said to be *in parity*. A *parity bit* can be appended to each transmission to ensure the integrity of the received data. The transmitter calculates the value of a parity bit based on the number of logic 1s in the character. This parity bit is inserted between the most significant data bit and the stop bit. On reception of the stop bit the receiver generates a parity bit based on the number of logic 0s and logic 1s in the received character. If the two parity bits match, the received character is considered valid. If the parity bits do not match, the received character is considered to be in error, and appropriate steps must be taken to affect a retransmission of the bad data.

There are two ways to calculate the parity bit. *Even parity* sets or resets the parity bit to a level that guarantees that the total number of logic 1s transmitted is an even number. *Odd parity* works in a similar manner except that the parity bit is set or reset to guarantee that the total number of logic 1s transmitted is an odd number. As was true with baud rate, both the transmitter and receiver must agree on the type of parity to be employed before communication can commence. Figure 4.2 illustrates an ASCII NUL and DEL as they are sent with even and odd parity. Let's analyze each character stream:

(a) This is DEL sent with odd parity. Because DEL already contains an odd number of logic 1 bits (7), the parity bit is taken to a logic 0 level to maintain odd parity.

(b) This is NULL sent with odd parity. The NULL has no logic 1 bits. Zero is considered an even number, so the parity bit is taken to a logic 1 level to achieve odd parity.

(c) This is DEL sent with even parity. The parity bit is brought to a marking level to maintain an even number (8) of logic 1 bits.

(d) Finally, this is NULL sent with even parity by bringing the parity bit to a spacing level for a total of zero logic 1 bits.

If generating the correct logic level for the parity bit seems confusing, just remember that the receiver includes the parity bit along with all the data bits when the receive check parity is generated.

4.4 INTEGRATED CIRCUITS USED IN RS-232 INTERFACES

For over a decade, special ICs have been available that simplify the design and repair of RS-232 interfaces. A functional knowledge of these ICs is essential to the process of designing interface cables and troubleshooting communications problems.

With the exception of the microprocessor, the introduction of the *universal asynchronous receiver and transmitter* (UART) has had the greatest effect on the simplification of terminal, printer, and computer interface design. "Universal" implies that the IC is fully programmable and is therefore, suitable to any RS-232

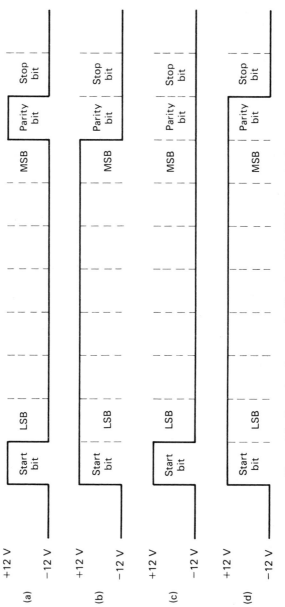

Figure 4.2 Examples of even and odd parity with ASCII NUL and DEL.

interface design. The programmable features of most UARTs include baud rate, number of data bits, number of start bits, number of stop bits, type of parity, manipulation of output handshaking lines, and sensing of input handshaking lines. The UART is both a transmitter (remember TD, pin 2, on the RS-232 connector) and a receiver (RD, pin 3). In this section we examine a generalized block diagram of a UART and discuss typical programming options.

Figure 4.3 depicts the block diagram of a generalized UART. The UART is powered by +5 V and ground. All the inputs and outputs meet standard TTL logic level specifications. This ensures that the UART can be *directly connected* to microprocessor circuitry. RS-232 transmitters and receivers are studied in the next section. Those devices provide the conversion between TTL and RS-232 voltage levels. Let's examine each block to discover how the UART interfaces to the world of the DTE's microprocessor controller and the RS-232 drivers and transmitters.

Important note.   A small *bubble* depicted in a schematic or block diagram indicates a line that is active at a logic 0 level. A bubbled input is active, or enabled, at a logic 0 and inactive, or disabled, at logic 1. A bubbled output indicates a symbolic inverter that *complements* the normal state of the output. We see examples of

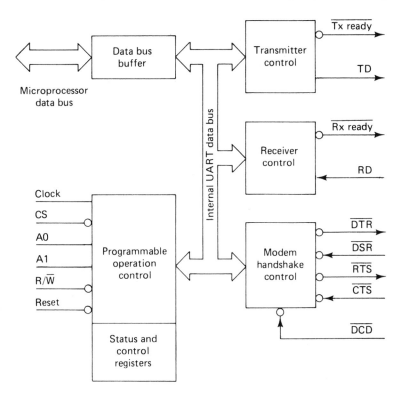

Figure 4.3   Block diagram of a UART.

bubbled inputs and outputs in the following discussion. Another indicator of active-low inputs and outputs is a long bar over the name or description of a line.

Data bus buffer.   The *data bus buffer* isolates the DTE's data bus from the internal data bus of the UART. All complex ICs that interface with a data bus have a similar type of buffer.

Programmable operation control.   This block of circuitry provides the means to program the various features of the UART and read status information concerning the handshaking lines on the interface.

Clock.   The *clock pin* is an input that is driven by an external clock generator IC. In digital circuits, clock signals are used to synchronize system operation, but most important to the UART, the clock is used as a time reference. This clock input is usually 16 times the baud rate. During the interval of 1 bit cell, the clock input will have 16 evenly spaced pulses. Remember that after a start bit is sensed, the receiver will wait for half a bit cell and then resample the line. This 16-times baud rate clock input enables the UART to sample the receive line precisely and to transmit the output bit stream with equally precise timing.

CS.   Although there are many intelligent ICs in a computer system, a microprocessor is capable of conversing with only one device at a time. The microprocessor selects the UART by pulling its *chip select* (CS) to an *active-low* level. This action is accomplished by qualifying the address outputs of the microprocessor by a TTL IC called an *address decoder*. Each I/O device in the computer system is assigned a unique address or range of addresses in which its CS is driven active.

Address lines

A0 and A1.   The most significant address outputs of the microprocessor are used to generate the various CS signals. The least significant address outputs are used to address a *register* (internal storage area) within the selected I/O device. In Figure 4.3, A0 and A1 are used to address one of four ($2^2 = 4$) internal locations within the UART.

Typical registers in a UART are as follows.

Transmit data-holding register.   Stores the output data as it is processed through the parallel-in–serial-out shift register.

Receive data holding register.   Stores the receive character after it is reassembled by the serial-in–parallel-out shift register.

Mode registers.   One or two registers that store the commands written by the microprocessor. These commands define the UART's *mode of operation.* Typical parameters are baud rate, number of start bits, number of data bits, number of stop bits, type of parity, and clock-to-baud-rate factor (which is usually 16, as discussed in the previous paragraph).

Command register.   This register is used to enable the transmitter and receiver and to control the handshaking outputs of DTR and RTS.

Status register.   The bits in the status register indicate the current operating status of the transmitter, receiver, and the state of the handshaking input lines: DCD, DSR, and CTS.

R/W.   When the *R/W* input is a logic 1 and the CS is active at a logic 0, the contents of the register addressed by A0 and A1 are placed on the outputs of the data buffer bus and read by the microprocessor. The microprocessor performs a read operation on the UART to obtain the byte of data from either the receive data holding register or the status register.

When R/W is at a logic 0 level and CS is asserted (logic 0) the byte of data residing on the inputs of the data bus buffer will be written into the register addressed by A0 and A1. The microprocessor performs a write operation on the UART to send a character to the transmit holding register or to program the UART with a mode or command byte.

Reset.   The active-low *reset* input resets the UART to a set of default parameters. This is usually accomplished when power is first applied to the computer, terminal, or printer.

We have just examined all the lines of the UART that are connected to the microprocessor side of the interface, as they appear on the left side of Figure 4.3. We must now consider the UART's connection with the RS-232 interface.

Transmitter control.   This block contains the transmit-data-holding register and the parallel-in–serial-out shift register.

Tx ready.   Tx ready is an active-low signal that can be used to indicate to the microprocessor that the transmit-data-holding register is empty and available to receive another character of transmit data. The status register has a bit of data that contains the same information as this output. That means the microprocessor can sense status through a hardware line (Tx ready) or through a software read operation (status register). Both methods are commonly employed.

TD.   The TTL level serial bit stream is output from the *TD* pin.

Receiver control.   The *receiver control* block contains the receive-data-holding register and the serial-in–parallel-out shift register.

Rx ready.   Rx ready is the receiver's equivalent of Tx ready. It goes active-low to indicate that the receive data holding register has a character for the microprocessor to read. A bit in the status register contains the same information. As we saw with Tx ready, receiver status can be derived through this hardware pin or through a microprocessor read operation of the status register.

RD.   *RD* is the TTL level input for the bit stream coming from the RS-232 receiver.

Modem handshake control.   The *modem handshake control* block manages the RS-232 handshake lines. It is interesting to notice that every line is active-low. Active-low inputs and outputs are dominant in TTL circuits. A confusion factor pertaining to active-low signals is that a logic 0 in TTL is a low voltage and a logic 0 in RS-232 is a high voltage. Remember that the UART is a TTL level device. A logic 0 applied to the input of DCD is generated from an RS-232 logic 0 as derived by the voltage translating RS-232 receiver.

DTR and RTS.   *DTR* and *RTS* are the two standard DTE handshake outputs. They are *set* (taken to a logic 1) or *reset* (taken to a logic 0) by writing to the appropriate bit in the command register.

DCD, CTS, and DSR.   *DCD, CTS,* and *DSR* are the three standard DTE handshake inputs controlled by the DCE (usually symbolized as the modem).

Remember that an active DCD line indicates that the local modem has sensed the carrier tone of another modem, implying that a remote connection has been achieved. On many UARTs the receiver will be enabled only when DCD at is an active-low level. On other UARTs the condition of this bit is monitored by reading the status register. The program is then free to interpret the state of DCD in any manner that it deems fit.

You should remember the function of CTS. The modem brings CTS low to indicate that its carrier is active and it is ready to transmit data. In many UARTs, CTS must be a logic 0 before the transmitter is enabled. In other UARTs, the state of CTS is read from the status register and is open to interpretation by the controlling program.

DSR is used as a general-purpose handshaking input. It is often the case that both DCD and DSR must be active before the UART will transmit data. Yet other times this input is completely ignored.

The actual pinout and names of pins on UARTs vary greatly, but the basic concepts explored in this section are applicable to all commercially available UARTs.

4.5 RS-232 DRIVERS AND RECEIVERS

RS-232 drivers and receivers accomplish the TTL-to-RS-232 and RS-232-to-TTL voltage translation process. We will now examine the two most popular driver and receiver ICs.

4.5.1 The MC1488 Quad Line Driver

As illustrated in Figure 4.4(a), this 14-pin IC contains four TTL to RS-232 line drivers. The output of any IC designated as a *line driver* differs from a standard output in that it is optimized to drive long, highly capacitive transmission lines.

The MC1488 requires two power-supply voltages, which are usually $+12$ V for $+V_{CC}$ and -12 V for $-V_{CC}$; signal ground is applied to pin 7. This leaves 11 pins to function as inputs and outputs. Three of the drivers are symbolized by two-input NAND gates. (A NAND gate is equivalent to an AND gate followed by an inverter). Because of the 11-pin limitation the fourth driver is symbolized as a one-input NAND gate.

Figure 4.4(b) illustrates the function table of the MC1488. Lines 1 through 3 indicate that if a logic 0 is placed on either input of the driver, the output will be an

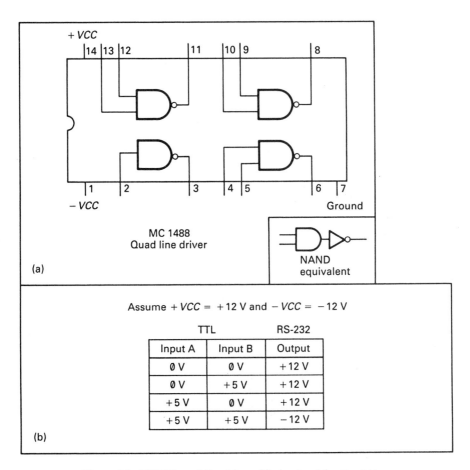

(a)

MC 1488
Quad line driver

NAND
equivalent

Assume $+VCC = +12$ V and $-VCC = -12$ V

TTL		RS-232
Input A	Input B	Output
0 V	0 V	+12 V
0 V	+5 V	+12 V
+5 V	0 V	+12 V
+5 V	+5 V	-12 V

(b)

Figure 4.4 MC1488 quad line driver—IC pinout and function table.

RS-232 logic 0 level of $+12$ V. When both inputs are equal to logic 1, the output will be -12 V, which is an RS-232 logic 1.

Many people find the operation of these two-input TTL to RS-232 drivers to be confusing. Two common questions are as follows.

1. Why should a driver have two inputs instead of just one?
2. Where does the inversion process symbolized by the bubble on the NAND gate occur? It appears that a TTL logic 0 will yield an RS-232 logic 0, and a TTL logic 1 will yield an RS-232 logic 1.

Figures 4.5 and 4.6 explain how the two inputs of the driver are employed. Figure 4.5(a) shows the function table of a NAND gate. The first and last lines of the function table indicate the case where both inputs are equal to the same value. Those two cases reveal an important characteristic of NAND gates:

When all the inputs of a NAND are tied together,

it behaves exactly like an inverter.

Most applications employing MC1488 drivers simply tie the two inputs together, as illustrated in Figure 4.5(b). The function table in Figure 4.5(b) is directly derived from the function table in Figure 4.4(b).

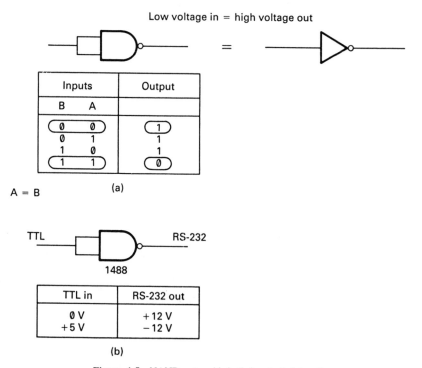

Figure 4.5 NAND gate with both inputs tied together.

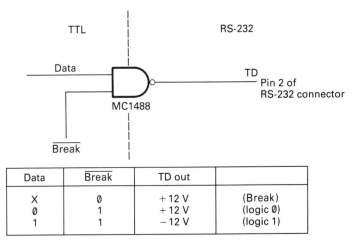

Data	Break	TD out	
X	0	+ 12 V	(Break)
0	1	+ 12 V	(logic 0)
1	1	− 12 V	(logic 1)

Figure 4.6   Data enable circuit used with an MC1488.

Figure 4.6 demonstrates an application that uses both pins of the MC1488 driver. The function table contains columns for two inputs and the TD RS-232 output. The first column indicates the state of the data transmitted by the UART. The break line is driven by other circuitry that creates a long duration spacing level called a "break condition" as described in Chapter 5.

Examine the first line of the function table. When break is at an active-low level, an X is entered under the data column. The X designates a *don't care* condition. When break is low, the RS-232 output is in a break condition. The second two lines of the function table describe normal data flow when break is inactive.

The second question that was posed concerned the inversion implied by the NAND gate, which does not actually appear to happen. In TTL the low voltage (0 V) is a logic 0 and the high voltage (+ 5 V) is a logic 1. In RS-232 the opposite is true—a low voltage (− 12 V) is a logic 1 and a high voltage (+ 12 V) is a logic 0. The inversion accomplished by the NAND gate transforms a low voltage (0 V) into a high voltage (+ 12 V) and a high voltage (+ 5 V) into a low voltage (− 12 V); although a voltage inversion occurs, the logic levels translated by the driver do not change. If RS-232 interpreted logic levels in the same manner as TTL, then a logic inversion would indeed occur.

4.5.2 The MC1489 RS-232 Quad Line Receiver

The MC1489 is a line receiver that converts RS-232 voltage levels into a TTL voltage levels. A *line receiver* is a device with special circuitry that is optimized to receive distorted digital signals from a long and highly capacitive transmission line.

Figure 4.7 illustrates the pinout and function table of the MC1489 RS-232-to-TTL line receiver. The inversion bubble on the inverter implies the same voltage inversion that we discussed concerning the MC1488. The inputs in the middle of each line receiver are used to control the receiver's response curve. In the great majority of applications, this pin is left open and can be ignored. In Chapter 8 we examine a serial interface board that employs these pins to modify the receiver's response curve.

The MC1489 provides the complementary operation of the MC1488. Because it translates RS-232 voltages to TTL voltages, it requires only $+5$ V DC power and ground.

4.5.3 Troubleshooting Driver and Receiver Malfunctions

There are many questions that must be answered concerning typical malfunctions of drivers and receivers. These questions consider the situations where driver or receiver lines are *floating* (open or unconnected) due to breaks in the circuit traces or broken wires in the interface, the effect of two driver outputs that are shorted together, and the state of the input handshaking lines when the interface is not connected to the RS-232 transmission line. These questions and many others are discussed in detail in Chapter 8.

Together with the UART, the line driver and line receiver constitute the circuitry in the serial interface. Figure 4.8 summarizes the UART-driver-receiver RS-232 interface.

These important concepts summarize the material in Chapter 4:

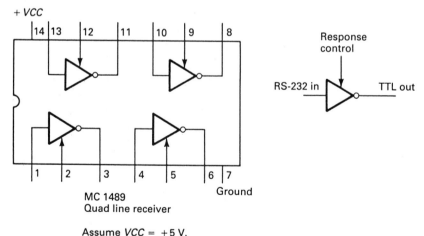

Figure 4.7 MC1489 quad line receiver pinout and function table.

- Asynchronous means "without regard to time." In asynchronous RS-232 communication, characters are sent at irregular intervals, not in a steady or continuous stream.
- Baud rate describes the speed at which each bit is transmitted.
- The inverse of the baud rate is the length of 1 bit cell.
- The transmission of each character in asynchronous communications is preceded by a start bit.
- The least significant data bit is transmitted first, followed by the remaining bits.
- Sampling each bit cell in the center eliminates the errors caused by the ringing that occurs each time a square wave switches logic levels.

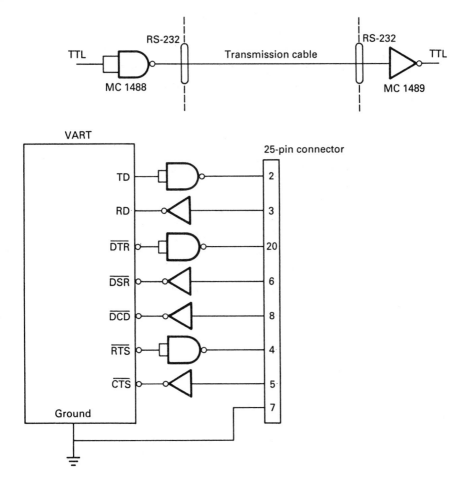

Figure 4.8   Driver and receiver circuitry of RS-232 interface.

- The stop bit is a marking level indicating that all the data bits have been sent.
- The start bit and stop bit create the bookends that constitute the character frame.
- A framing error occurs if the receiver is looking for a stop bit but senses a logic 0 level.
- Parity is employed to detect single bit errors.
- The parity bit appears in the bit stream after the most significant data bit and before the stop bit.
- Even or odd parity can be selected during the setup of an RS-232 device.
- The UART is a programmable receiver-transmitter used to interface the parallel world of microprocessor systems with the serial world of RS-232 communications.
- The introduction of the UART has had a major effect in simplifying the design and reducing the cost of terminals, printers, and other RS-232 peripherals.
- Progammable features of most UARTs include the number of data bits, number of stop bits, baud rate, parity, and hardware handshaking considerations.
- UARTs contain status registers that may be interrogated by a program to determine the condition of the DCE handshaking lines.
- UARTs contain command registers, which the driver software programs use to control the communications parameters of the UART and the DTE handshaking lines.
- Line drivers are used to convert the TTL level bit stream from the UART into RS-232 voltage levels.
- Line drivers are optimized to drive long capacitive transmission lines.
- Line receivers are used to convert RS-232 level bit streams into TTL voltage levels that can be processed by the UART.
- Line receivers are optimized to receive degraded signals from long, highly capacitive transmission lines.
- The response input on line receivers is usually left floating (open or unconnected.)

5

RS-232 Terminals and Microcomputer Terminal Emulation

The first four chapters of this book have laid the foundation for a successful understanding of the setup, operation, and interface cable design of actual RS-232 devices. We now examine RS-232 asynchronous terminals and microcomputers used as terminals with emulation software.

5.1 CHARACTER GENERATION ON VIDEO DISPLAYS

Characters produced by handwriting and typewriters are continuous; they are constructed from unbroken lines. The characters created on video displays and by dot-matrix printers are not continuous but are constructed from groups of adjacent dots. Figure 5.1 illustrates the typical rectangular matrix used to generate high-quality characters on video displays.

Letters, numerals, and special symbols are created by illuminating (or printing) selected dots in the rectangular matrix. The perfect dot-matrix character appears to be continuous, not actually a product of a finite number of dots. The major factors that affect the readability of dot-matrix characters are the size of each dot, the number of dots in the character matrix, and the distance between each dot. A comparison of a 7×9 dot-matrix character and a 5×7 dot-matrix character of equal physical size reveals that the first character is appreciably more readable and less fatiguing to the eye. The second character not only has fewer dots, but the dots must also be larger or farther apart to constitute an equal-size character.

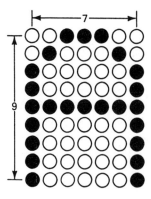

Figure 5.1 The letter *A* as constructed from a 7 × 9 dot matrix.

Each character is enclosed in a *character box*. The character box provides space between adjacent characters in the same row and on different lines. It also affords room for lowercase letters to descend below the base line of uppercase characters. Lowercase letters created in such a fashion are called *true descenders*. On early video displays lowercase letters were not true descenders but appeared on the same horizontal plane as uppercase characters.

Figure 5.2(a) illustrates the screen capacity of a typical video display. Each row contains a maximum of 80 characters. The first 24 rows are used to display standard text, whereas the last row is usually reserved for special information regarding terminal status or applications information. Figure 5.2(b) is a magnified examination of the five characters displayed in Figure 5.2(a). Each character is constructed from a 7 × 9 dot matrix and is enclosed in a 9 × 14 character box. For a terminal utilizing this 9 × 14 character box, the screen capacity can be redefined as 720 dots (80 characters times 9 dots per character) by 350 dots (25 rows times 14 dots per character).

The process of painting characters on a video display is similar to the process of painting a field of video information on a television. A CRT is constructed from an electron gun, horizontal and vertical deflection coils (called the *yoke*), and a phosphor-coated screen that glows when stuck by electrons. The electron gun fires electrons at the screen of the CRT. It is "aimed" by the magnetic fields produced by the vertical and horizontal deflection coils in the yoke assembly. The electron beam is initially aimed at the upper left-hand corner of the screen—first column in the first row of dots. The top row of each character is painted by moving the electron beam from left to right.

When the electron beam reaches the last dot in the first row, a signal called *horizontal sync* is asserted. Horizontal sync *blanks* (turns off) the electron beam and returns it to the first column in the second row of dots. The second row of dots is painted in a similar fashion. It takes 14 sweeps of the electron beam to paint the first line of 80 characters. This process continues until the last column in the last row is painted. A signal called *vertical sync* is then asserted. Vertical sync blanks the electron beam and returns it to the upper left-hand corner of the screen and the process

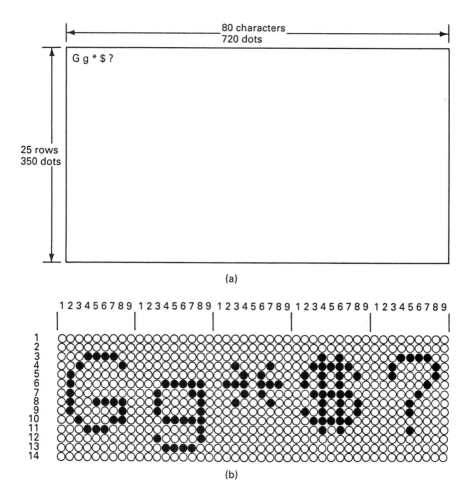

(a)

(b)

Figure 5.2 Screen capacity and dot generation of characters.

of painting the *frame* of video information is repeated. The *persistence* of the human eye is such that the screen must be *refreshed* at least 50 to 60 times each second to avoid detecting the flicker produced by the painting process.

The process of painting a frame of 2000 characters requires many specialized ICs. The heart of the video subsystem is a complex programmable IC called a *CRT controller*. One or two bytes of *video refresh memory* (often called "display RAM") are required to hold the ASCII code of each character and any associated *character attributes* (such as blinking, underlined, reverse video, or intensified). The contents of the video refresh memory are changed as new characters are written to the video display.

A ROM called the *character generator* contains the bit patterns required to create each dot-matrix character. Finally, a parallel-in–serial-out shift register is used to transform the output of the character generator into a bit stream to bias the control grid of the electron gun. A logic 1 causes the electron gun to fire a sufficient number of electrons to illuminate a dot of the face of the CRT. A logic 0 suspends the firing of electrons, which results in a dark spot on the face of the CRT. In this manner the dot patterns of each character are painted onto the screen. Figure 5.3 is a block diagram that illustrates the relationships of the components in the video subsystem.

5.2 THE DIFFERENCE BETWEEN RS-232 TERMINALS AND VIDEO MONITORS

Before we can fully discuss terminals, we must take a moment to understand the difference between a standard RS-232 terminal and the video monitor that is employed by most microcomputers. Figure 5.4(a) illustrates the block diagram of an RS-232 terminal. A typical terminal consists of five units: a logic board, monitor board, power supply, CRT (which are contained in one enclosure), and a detachable keyboard.

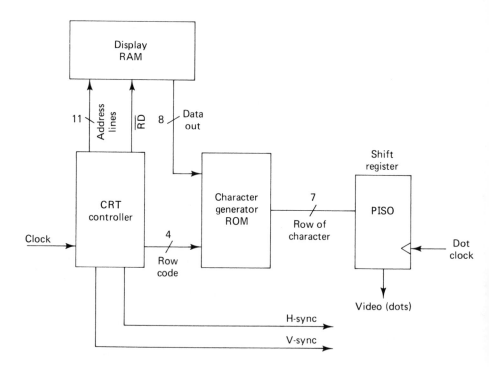

Figure 5.3 Block diagram of video subsystem.

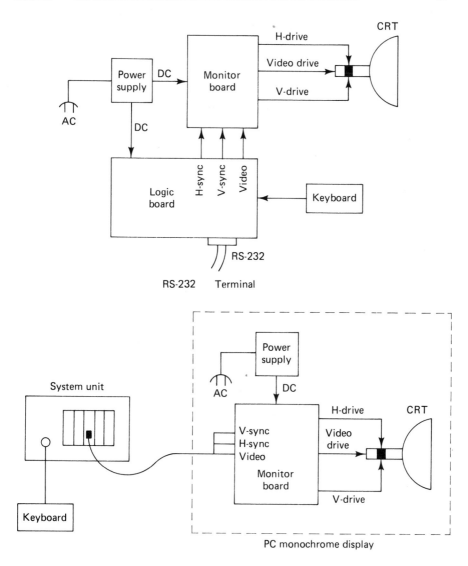

Figure 5.4   RS-232 terminal and microcomputer video monitor.

Logic board.   The circuitry on the logic board provides many functions:
Communications: The UART and RS-232 drivers and receivers constitute the communications circuitry used to connect the terminal with a computer via the RS-232 interface.

Video subsystem: The video subsystem illustrated in Figure 5.3 is also contained on the logic board.

Microprocessor controller: A microprocessor and ROMs continuously execute routines that control the communications circuitry, video subsystem, keyboard, and other complex system functions. ROMs that contain dedicated programs to control a microprocessor-based system are called *firmware*. This term is derived from the fact that although ROMs are ICs, which are classified as *hardware*, they also hold programs that are classified as *software*. The term *firmware* denotes hardware (ROMs) that contains dedicated software. Not all ROMs are classified as firmware. Certain ROMS (such as the character generator that we just examined) do not hold programs but only specific data.

Power supply.   The *power supply* (*P/S*) transforms, rectifies, and filters the AC line power into the DC voltages required to power the ICs and transistors on the logic board, keyboard, and monitor board.

Video monitor board.   The monitor board converts the digital signals of horizontal sync, vertical sync, and video information (created by the video subsystem on the logic board) into the analog signals required to drive the deflection coils and electron gun. The monitor board also holds the *fly-back transformer* and associated diodes that transform and rectify the voltage induced by the motion of moving the electron beam from the end of the line to the beginning of the next line (known as fly-back) into the 10-kV to 15-kV DC voltage required to power the anode of the electron gun.

CRT.   As we indicated in Section 5.1, the CRT subsystem contains the deflection coils, electron gun, and phosphor-coated screen.

Keyboard.   The keyboard is usually connected to a special I/O port on the logic board via a standard modular phone jack. It generally contains local intelligence in the form of a microprocessor and firmware that scans the keyboard looking for closed key switches. The microprocessor *debounces* (waits for normal mechanical bouncing to stop) the closed key and then transmits the *key code* to the microprocessor on the logic board. The keyboard often contains an audio speaker. When an ASCII Bel (§G) is sent to the terminal, the microprocessor on the logic board redirects the character to the microprocessor in the keyboard. The keyboard microprocessor then drives the speaker with a short audio frequency square wave.

In Chapter 1 we established the need for a widely accepted interface standard. That need was based on the motivation to create universal compatibility between computers and peripherals. The terminal illustrated in Figure 5.4(a) physically interfaces to the computer via the RS-232 serial port. From the interface's point of view all RS-232 devices look identical. A terminal connected to a computer does not see the internal workings of the computer but only a connection with a remote RS-232 port. The RS-232 standard creates this device-independent environment.

Now we must consider the block diagram of a typical video monitor used in microcomputers, as illustrated in Figure 5.4(b). The video monitor and terminal have three common subassemblies: a monitor board, power supply, and CRT. The logic board and keyboard are independent units. This means that video monitors must be designed to interface to a specific logic board—they do not possess the hardware independence enjoyed by RS-232 terminals.

The microcomputer's equivalent of a logic board is called a *video adapter board* and is housed within the *system unit* of the microcomputer. The keyboard plugs directly in a keyboard port on the system unit. Hardware independence is sacrificed for the ability to customize the video subsystem and keyboard for specific applications. The IBM-PC is an example of a microcomputer system in which dozens of keyboards, video adapter boards, and video monitors are available and widely employed.

RS-232 terminals and computers communicate in standard ASCII. Video monitors receive horizontal sync, vertical sync, and video information from a video adapter board plugged into the system unit. This allows microcomputers to have *bit-mapped graphics*. Instead of utilizing a character-generator ROM to create the 14 rows of 9 dots that define a character, bit-mapped graphics address each individual dot on the screen. In this way complex custom graphics can be produced. The applications program creates an infinite number of unique dot patterns instead of the set group of characters and block graphics that are found in character-generator ROMs.

Video adapter boards are available for the IBM-PC that provide standard character sets via a character-generator ROM but that can also be instructed to enter a special *all-points-addressable* (APA) mode in which bit-mapped graphics displays are created by writing bit patterns directly into the video refresh memory.

Later in this chapter we discuss how a microcomputer employing an RS-232 port can function as a standard RS-232 terminal. This allows the microcomputer user to have the best of both worlds—a flexible stand-alone work station and a vehicle to access large computer systems and communications networks.

5.3 TERMINAL SETUP PARAMETERS

In this section we examine the options that users must select before connecting a terminal to a modem or directly to a computer. Older terminals have two or more banks of DIP switches (accessible from the rear) that are used to select *setup parameters*. When the terminal is powered up, the microprocessor residing on the logic board reads the settings of the setup switches and configures the system appropriately.

Newer terminals have an internal setup program that is invoked by depressing a *setup key* on the keyboard. Related setup parameters are displayed on the 25th line of the terminal. The options for each field can be examined and set. A typical setup procedure has four to five lines of parameters. When the setup selection is complete, the parameters are saved in low-power RAM. This special RAM is powered by a battery when the terminal is turned off. Consequently, the setup is never lost and need be invoked only to change options. The system microprocessor reads the setup RAM in the same manner that the setup switches on older terminals are read to establish the terminal operational parameters. The following setup parameters are extremely common and need to be set correctly to ensure proper terminal operation.

Communications baud rate. The RS-232 port is labeled *communications, modem,* or *RS-232.* If your terminal is connected to a modem, you must select the baud rate that matches the speed of the modem.

Some computer ports are *auto-baud* ports. When a terminal is directly connected to an auto-baud port, the port waits for a terminal to assert DTR. This indicates that the computer port is connected to a functioning terminal. At that point, the user strikes the carriage-return key. The auto-baud port expects to see this CR character and derives the baud rate, number of data bits, and parity of the terminal from the bit stream. This convenient feature is found on many computer systems.

Typical baud rates for asynchronous modems are 300, 1200, and 2400 baud. Baud rates for directly connected terminals range from 1200 baud to 19,200 baud (19.2 kB). Widely used baud rates include 9600 and 4800. Remember that the capacitance of a transmission line is the major constraint limiting the maximum baud rate that can be employed before signal degradation and, as a result, communications errors occur.

Printer port baud rate. RS-232 terminals have a second RS-232 port that is labeled *AUX* (auxiliary), *printer,* or *extension.* This port is designed to be connected to a local printer. Unlike the communications port of the terminal, which is a DTE port, the printer port is a DCE port, and the terminal transmits data to the printer on pin 3. Printers are classified as DTEs. As you already know, DTEs are designed to communicate with DCEs. By having the printer port on a terminal perform the role of a DCE, a serial printer can be directly connected to the printer port.

In normal operation the printer port is disabled. It can be enabled remotely by having the computer send a special control code or escape sequence, or it can be enabled locally to print an image of the screen by striking the key usually labeled *print screen.* We discuss the various printer operation modes and typical baud rates later in this chapter.

Number of data bits per character. Standard ASCII is a 7-bit code. Some computers use an 8-bit code that contains an extra 128 characters for extended block graphics or foreign language character sets. Seven data bits is normal with minicomputers. Eight-bit characters are popular with multiuser microcomputer systems that employ standard RS-232 terminals.

Number of stop bits. One start bit is universally standard. Most terminals allow the user to select 1 or 2 stop bits. In the great majority of applications, 1 stop bit is used. Remember that the stop bit marks the end of the asynchronous character frame. The wrong number of stop bits will cause intermittent problems. We will discuss specific symptoms in Chapter 8.

Local and duplex modes.   When a terminal is in local mode, each key pressed is sent directly to the display but not to the UART for transmission. A terminal set to duplex will send the ASCII code for each key pressed to the UART for transmission. In popular computer terminology, local mode equates to *off-line* and duplex mode, to *on-line*. Here duplex is used to indicate two-party communication between a terminal and computer.

Full- or half-duplex modes.   Consider a terminal that is not connected to a modem or a computer. When a key is depressed, the character probably will not appear on the video display. Most terminals are configured to operate in *full-duplex modes*. This means that the ASCII code of a key pressed is transmitted on the TD pin of the RS-232 connector. When the computer receives the character, it *echoes* it back on the RD line. This guarantees that the computer and terminal are actually communicating.

In some applications the computer is not capable of echoing characters. In those situations the terminal is set up in *half-duplex mode*. When a key is depressed on a terminal operating in half-duplex, the ASCII code is sent out on TD and the character is written into the video refresh memory to be displayed by the video subsystem. The appearance of keystrokes on the video display of a terminal operating in half-duplex does not necessarily indicate that the terminal is actually communicating with a computer.

If each character typed on the keyboard appears twice on the display, the terminal is set for half-duplex and is connected onto a full-duplex line. If the terminal displays only characters originated by the computer, then the terminal is set for full-duplex and is communicating with a computer operating in half-duplex. We discuss further troubleshooting symptoms in Chapter 8.

The formal definitions of full-duplex and half-duplex pertain to the simultaneous transmission and reception of data and do not necessarily add any clarity to the concepts discussed in the previous paragraph. In full-duplex operation, a terminal can transmit and receive data simultaneously. In half-duplex operation a terminal can send or receive data but not both simultaneously. This is analogous to a conversation over a CB (citizens' band) transceiver. When one person is done talking (transmitting), he or she says "over" to indicate that the other party is now clear to transmit (and the first person switches to receive mode). Both full- and half-duplex conversations use separate lines for send and receive data. When communication occurs over a single line in only one direction, the connection is called a *simplex*. The definitions for these concepts have been included only for the sake of completeness.

Character or block mode.   Character mode designates conventional character-by-character communications in half- or full-duplex. When a terminal is set to block mode, the keys pressed by the operator will not be sent on the transmit data line but only echoed to the screen (as if the terminal were in local mode, as just described.) When the screen is full of information, a key—usually labeled *send*—is depressed, and the characters on the screen are transmitted in a continuous block. It is important to realize that although the characters are sent in a continuous block, each character is still framed by start and stop bits.

Block mode is also called *forms' mode.* Imagine the situation where puchase orders are entered into a computer. The terminal is set to block mode and the applications program sketches a purchase order form onto the video display; each blank on the form is completed by the operator, the entries are checked for accuracy, the send key is depressed, and the completed form is sent to the computer. This makes much more efficient use of the computer's resources than sending data on a high-overhead, character-by-character basis. Figure 5.5 summarizes half-duplex, full-duplex, and block modes.

Parity enable.   This setting enables or disables parity generation and checking.

Type of parity.   If parity is enabled, you must designate the type of parity employed by the host computer. We have already seen examples of even and odd parity. Some terminals offer the additional options of mark and space parity. Mark and space parity are not actual parity settings in the sense of error checking. They append the data stream with a logic 1 (mark parity) or logic 0 (space parity). They are used only in rare situations where the computer needs to see an extra bit at a specified level appended to the data stream.

If your terminal does not support mark or space parity but it is required by your computer system, use the following "trick." Assume that the computer wants to see 7 data bits, 1 stop bit, and mark parity. Simply set the terminal for 7 data bits, no parity, and 2 stop bits. The first stop bit (mark) will appear as mark parity. A 7-data bit, 1 stop bit, and space parity requirement is satisfied by setting the terminal to 8 data bits, no parity, and 1 stop bit. The logic 0 (space) in the eighth-data bit position appears as space parity.

Some computers support any type of parity, whereas others are set to a particular type of parity. On multiuser microcomputer systems each port can be programmed for a specific type of parity by the system administrator.

Emulation mode.   Although all RS-232 terminals are identical from an interface point of view, they implement different control and escape sequences to support sophisticated programming features. Many terminals can *emulate* popular types of terminals that are widely supported by computer systems. The ADM-3A by Lear Siegler, TVI 920-C by Televideo Inc., and the VT-100 by Digital Equipment Corporation (DEC) are popular emulation choices. You need to enter emulation mode if your terminal is not supported by a particular computer system, and you need to use an application that requires *cursor addressing* or other advanced features.

Normal or reverse video.   The *normal or reverse video* option enables you to choose light characters on a dark background (normal video) or dark charac-

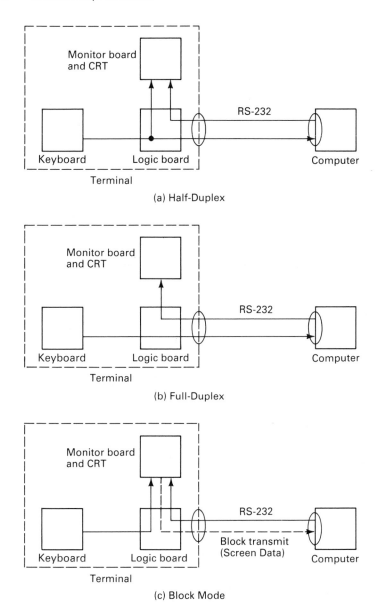

Figure 5.5   Half-duplex, full-duplex, and block mode.

ters on a light background (reverse video). On the great majority of terminals, reverse video is fatiguing on the eyes and is used only as a special effect to highlight
important data.

Refresh rate.   The refresh rate of a terminal designates the frequency of the video display refresh cycle (the time between vertical sync pulses). This rate must match the AC line frequency. In the United States and Canada this is 60 Hz; in Europe it is 50 Hz. If the refresh rate is set incorrectly, the display will quiver and appear unfocused, or fuzzy. As an experiment, try setting the refresh rate incorrectly so you will recognize the symptom in the future.

CR or CR/LF.   Remember that a CR character returns the cursor to the first column in the current line. Most computer systems will echo an LF character in addition to each CR; other systems will not append the LF. In that case a complete *CR/LF* sequence must be generated by the terminal.

   If the text on a terminal is double-spaced, the CR/LF is enabled at the terminal and the computer is also sending an LF, resulting in two LFs for each CR. If a terminal displays only one line of text that is continually written over, CR/LF is disabled and the computer is not sending an LF with the echoed CR.

Monitor mode enable.   Many terminals support a *monitor mode*. In this mode a special character-generator ROM creates the characters used to symbolize the first 32 control codes in ASCII. It is important to understand that in monitor mode, control codes and escape sequences are displayed but not executed as commands by the terminal. A CR received in monitor mode is displayed as a lowercase *c* above a lowercase *r*, all in one character box, but the cursor is not returned to the beginning of the current line. Monitor mode is extremely helpful in debugging programs that send complex control and escape sequences to the terminal.

Terminal self-test.   The firmware on the logic board contains self-tests that verify correct terminal operation. There are three varieties of self-tests. Each time a terminal is powered on, the microprocessor runs a *power-on self-test*. Most terminals will simply beep and display the cursor to indicate that the power-on self-test passed; others display a start-up message and terminal logo. If your terminal displays a cursor but does not beep on power-up, confirm that the keyboard is connected. (Remember that the speaker is most often in the keyboard.)

   The two other self-tests are invoked from the keyboard, the setup switches, or the setup menu. An *internal self-test* displays the terminal's complete character set and attributes. This checks everything except for the keyboard and the communications circuitry.

   To perform the *external self-test,* a *loop-back* is installed on the modem port of the terminal. Figure 5.6 illustrates the connections of the loop-back plug. TD and RD are shorted together. The external self-test transmits the complete character set. The data leaving TD is routed into RD, where it is received and displayed. This test verifies the operation of the UART and the RS-232 drivers and receivers. The terminal thinks it is attached to a modem or computer because of the loop-back connections on the handshaking pins. The terminal asserts RTS, which is connected to CTS. The terminal also asserts DTR, which is connected to DCD and DSR. This guarantees that the UART is enabled for the transmission and reception of data.

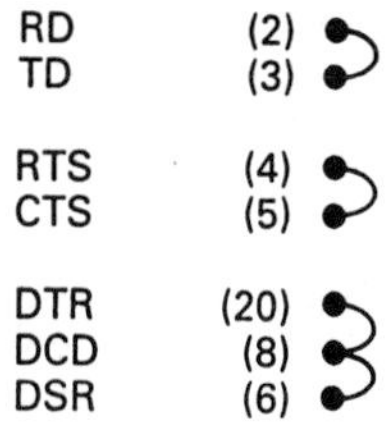

```
                               RD      (2)
                               TD      (3)

                               RTS     (4)
                               CTS     (5)

                               DTR     (20)
Figure  5.6  Loop-back plug used for ex-   DCD   (8)
ternal terminal test.          DSR     (6)
```

Figure 5.6 Loop-back plug used for external terminal test.

The loop-back plug can be used to test the keyboard (and terminal operation in general) of a terminal set in full-duplex by simply plugging it into the modem port and typing a message that uses all of the letters in the alphabet. ''The quick brown fox jumped over the lazy dog'' is a favorite phrase for testing keyboards. We learn more about troubleshooting systems in Chapter 8.

Other options.   Other popular options allow the user to set the type of cursor (block, underline, blinking, or steady), force the video display to blank out after a specified length of inactivity (this increases the life of the phosphor on the CRT), enable or disable a key click sound to accompany each keystroke, set hardware handshaking attributes on the modem and printer ports, and enable or disable the 25th line of the display to show terminal status.

When the baud rate of a terminal is set so fast (9600 or 19200 baud) that the scrolling of the video display cannot keep pace with the incoming data, terminals usually default to X-ON/X-OFF flow control. When the video refresh RAM is in danger of being overrun, the terminal sends an X-OFF character, and the computer suspends data transmission. When the scrolling catches up with the data in the video refresh RAM, an X-ON character is transmitted to the computer and normal data transmission is resumed.

Most printers support both X-ON/X-OFF flow control and hardware handshaking on DTR. As an alternative to handshaking on pin 20 (DTR), some printers handshake on pin 11 of the RS-232 interface. The printer ports on terminals usually reserve both pins 20 and 11 for hardware handshaking. It is important to read the printer's documentation closely to reveal how it handshakes and then set the terminal accordingly. We discuss printers in the next chapter.

5.4 PROGRAMMING TERMINALS

A *driver* is a low-level program (usually written is assembly language) that is used to control a specific I/O device. The control codes and escape sequences utilized by terminals differ greatly between models and manufacturers. Thus each different type of terminal supported by a computer system must have an appropriate *terminal driver program*. When you log into a mini- or mainframe computer, the computer usually asks for your terminal type. This enables the computer to filter its commands through the correct driver program. Many options selected in the setup switches can be changed under program control by sending the appropriate control code or escape sequence.

Let's examine some typical commands used to control the output on terminal displays.

Cursor control.   An important feature of terminals is the ability to move the cursor directly to any location on the screen. This functionality is required by full-screen editors (word-processing-type programs), programs that employ forms, such as data-base management systems, and game programs, where a game piece must be moved on a board without overwriting the other pieces. We already know the control codes to move the cursor up, down, left, and right. To move the cursor directly to any location on the screen usually involves an escape character followed by a command letter and the row and column address of the location to place the cursor.

The cursor-positioning sequence for an ADM-3A terminal requires four characters and is of the following general form:

```
ESC  =  column, row
```

The ESC and = characters are followed by the appropriate codes to define the destination column and row position. The 4-byte 1B, 3D, 33, 24 hex sequence will move the cursor from its current position to the twentieth column of the fifth row on the video display. Refer to your terminal programming manual for the actual commands.

In the same manner that a cursor can be directly placed at any location on the screen, the current location of the cursor can be read by a program using the appropriate escape sequence.

Defining visual attributes.   Special attributes such as normal, blinking, reverse video, highlighted, half intensity, or any combination of those can be associated with one or more characters.

Setting tab positions.   We know that an HT character causes the cursor to move to the next tab stop on the current line. Every terminal has a mechanism to define locations of the tab stops.

Clearing screen or lines.   Commands are available to clear the whole screen of characters or just a line or portion of a line.

Protected fields.   In the last section you learned about block mode and forms. If a program paints a form onto the display, there must be a means of protecting the form from being overwritten by a careless user. Particular parts of the display can be set to protected mode. This ensures that the form is not accidentally destroyed.

Printer modes. There are many different ways to enable a local printer connected to the auxiliary port on the terminal. If the screen contains information that must be copied by the printer, a page print command can be executed. This dumps the contents of the video refresh memory into the printer port.

Transparent print mode redirects the output of the computer from the computer screen to the printer. *Extension print mode* sends the computer's output to both the screen and the printer. *Bidirectional print mode* electrically places the modem port and printer port in parallel.

In all these modes the printer can be enabled to handshake with X-ON/X-OFF or by DTR to indicate a buffer full condition. In many terminals the baud rate of the modem port and printer port must be the same except in the page print mode. In other terminals the baud rates of the modem port and printer port need never be the same. Carefully read your terminal operator's manual to understand how these print modes are implemented.

Break key. Most terminal keyboards have a *break key*. Unlike the other keys, depressing the break key does not cause an ASCII character to be transmitted but rather a long-duration spacing level (usually 250 ms). The UART or other hardware in the computer's interface port detects this break condition. The break key is used to indicate that an unrecoverable error has occurred and the operator's keyboard is essentially locked up. Most computers perform a software reset on the terminal's port that originated the break condition.

5.5 MICROCOMPUTER TERMINAL EMULATION

If you are one of the millions of people who owns a microcomputer, do you need a separate RS-232 terminal to dial up computer systems and electronic bulletin boards? Absolutely not! Almost all micros are supported by communications programs that provide three services: communications, terminal emulation, and file transfer.

The communications module provides the functionality to set the baud rate, number of data bits, number of stop bits, parity, and other common terminal parameters. Entering setup mode, the applications program writes a setup menu to the video display. By moving the cursor to a particular parameter, the possible choices can be viewed. The setup is saved on the disk drive and need not be accomplished each time the program is invoked. Teamed with the RS-232 port on the microcomputer, the communications module enables the microcomputer to function as a *dumb terminal*. Dumb terminals do not have sophisticated programmable features. They cannot be used with any program that requires full-screen cursor addressing. Basically, dumb terminals behave exactly like old teletypes; they process data in a line-by-line manner. For that reason, dumb terminals are often described as *glass TTYs*. Most electronic communications services, on-line data bases, and bulletin boards default to dumb terminal as the terminal type when the user logs on.

The second module enables the microcomputer to emulate a popular terminal. To accomplish this emulation, the communications program must translate the control codes and escape sequences sent by the remote computer into commands that the microcomputer's hardware can execute. As was true with the emulation operations in terminals, the ADM-3A, TVI-920, and VT-100 are popular emulation choices.

The third module addresses an extremely important aspect of microcomputer communications. Consider the situation where a large *data base* is stored on the disk drives of a mainframe computer. Suppose we dial into a computer that has a data base of articles written on the subject of energy conservation. After setting up the correct communications parameters, a modem is employed to dial up the remote computer. As we log into the system the terminal emulation module enables us to identify ourselves as a popular terminal. We can now search the data base for articles of interest.

How do we get a *hard copy* of a particular article? The third module in a microcomputer communications program supports file-transfer operations. In this example we want to transfer the date file from the mainframe computer onto the disk of our local microcomputer. This is called *down-loading* a file. The complementary operation of transferring a file from our local microcomputer to a mainframe is called *up-loading* a file.

There are two methods of supporting computer-to-computer file transfer. The simplest technique is called *data-capture, data-collection,* or *raw-transfer* mode. Recall the situation where we want to down-load a file from a remote data base. Using data-capture, we simply instruct the computer to save all the incoming data in a file of a specified name as well as displaying it on the video display. At the conclusion of the file transmission, an escape sequence is entered from the keyboard that instructs the local computer to close the new file and terminate data-capture mode. The new file is then inspected and edited for extraneous or incidental information.

The beauty of data-capture file transfer is its utter simplicity. There are two glaring deficiencies:

1. The file must be edited to remove incidental information that was transmitted by the computer system while the microcomputer was gathering data.
2. Data-capture file transfer does absolutely no error checking. Simply parity checking is not sufficient—there is no guarantee that the captured data written into the file has not been corrupted.

The second form of file-transfer utility employs a sophisticated *communications protocol.* This protocol defines the manner in which the data is sent and checked for errors and how transmission status is acknowledged by the receiving computer. Let's examine the file-transfer protocol of a popular communications program called *Kermit.* Kermit was developed at Columbia University in New York City and is now in the *public domain.* Public domain programs are available from computer-user groups, electronic bulletin boards, and universities for the cost of a floppy disk. Kermit is supported on more micro, mini, and mainframe computers than any other communications program.

Kermit is executed just like any other program by typing its name followed by a carriage return. This takes the user to the Kermit command level. Here local commands can be issued, such as set baud rate, parity, number of data bits, and so on. The process of preparing to send a file or receive a file is also handled at the Kermit command level.

After the required communications parameters are set, the *connect* command is executed and Kermit enters terminal emulation mode. The microcomputer now functions as a standard ASCII terminal. The connection with a remote mainframe computer is achieved, and the user can proceed with the normal log-in procedure. (Different versions of Kermit emulate different types of terminals. You must refer to the Kermit documentation to know what terminal your micro is emulating.)

Now that we are logged into a remote computer, let's examine the process of down-loading a file. The command *Kermit s (filename)* informs the host computer that a file named (filename) will be down-loaded (*s* stands for send) to the microcomputer. The user then escapes to the Kermit command level with a ˆ]c sequence and executes the command *receive*, which causes the microcomputer to enter the down-load file transfer mode. The transfer commences and Kermit provides file-transfer statistics, such as the number of bytes, data packets received, and the number of transmission errors and retries.

The file-transfer operation can be somewhat confusing because part of the time the micro acts as a terminal and at other times it acts as a computer. When the down-load operation is first invoked, the micro acts as a terminal. When the user escapes back to the Kermit command level, the micro is then acting as a computer and runs the file-transfer program, which is a portion of Kermit. After the transfer is complete and the user types *connect,* the micro once again emulates a terminal. It is important to realize that during the actual file-transfer process, both computers are running their own versions of the Kermit file-transfer program.

Figure 5.7 illustrates the *Kermit packet.* A *packet* is a block of related data. In the Kermit file-transfer protocol, all information that passes between the sender and receiver is in the form of the Kermit packet in Figure 5.7. Each packet is broken into *fields* of data.

Mark field.   The *mark* is usually a ˆA, which designates an ASCII *SOH* (start-of-header control character). The mark is the only field that contains a nonprintable ASCII character. This assures that none of the information in the other fields is accidentally interpreted as a control command by the receiver.

Length field.   Kermit packets are of variable length. The *length field* indicates the number of bytes in the current packet.

Mark	Len	Seq	Type	Data	Check

Figure 5.7   A Kermit packet.

Sequence field. The *sequence field* is used to detect lost or duplicate packets. The packets in a file-transfer operation are numbered in sequential order. If the receiver detects an error in a packet, it requests the retransmission of the specific packet number. If the receiver senses the transmission of a duplicate packet, that data is ignored.

Type field. There are two types of files. Standard ASCII *text files* consist of printable ASCII characters with codes between 20H and 7FH. *Object code* or *binary files* consist of arbitrary bit patterns. These files may be executable programs or specially encoded information. Because Kermit wants to send only printable ASCII characters in all fields (with the exception of the mark), these binary files must be converted into standard text files by the transmitter and then reconverted into binary files by the receiver. The *type field* indicates which type of data is contained in the current packet.

Data field. The *data field* contains the ASCII data for the text files or the encoded ASCII for binary files. This is where the actual information resides. The rest of the packet is purely overhead and exists only to support the reliable transfer of the data field.

Check field. The *check field* contains a *checksum* or *CRC* (cyclic redundancy check) that is calculated by the transmitter and sent as the last field in the packet. The receiver calculates an equivalent checksum or CRC and compares it against the received value. If the two disagree, the receiver notifies the sender that the packet must be retransmitted. The check field is the logical extension of the parity bit that we have studied for detecting single bit errors in asynchronously transmitted ASCII characters.

A typical Kermit file transfer operation proceeds as follows:

The sender transmits a send-initialize packet that contains specific parameters describing the packet.

The receiver responds with an *ACK* (acknowledgment packet). The ACK signifies that the first packet was received correctly, and it also describes its own packet parameters.

The sender transmits a file-header packet containing the name of the file that will be transferred in the data field.

The receiver ACKs the file-header packet.

The sender now transmits packets containing actual file-transfer data in the data field, and the receiver ACKs a correctly received packet or *NAKs* (negative acknowledge packet) an incorrectly received packet as determined by the check field. A NAK contains the sequence number of the packet that must be retransmitted.

The Kermit protocol results in an extremely reliable form of asynchronous data transfer that works on most micro-, mini-, and mainframe computers. We have only overviewed the complete protocol. Columbia University publishes many documents, including the *Kermit User's Guide* and the *Kermit Protocol Manual*. These documents are a must for those who want to understand all the aspects of the communications program and the intricacies of the protocol.

One of the oldest and still widely employed file-transfer protocols in the public domain is called *X-modem*. This protocol is supported by many communications packages and by most electronic bulletin boards and information sources. Because it is public domain (as is Kermit), X-modem is a must for all microcomputer users who want to transfer files and programs between many different systems. Contact your local electronic bulletin board for information on obtaining a copy of X-modem that will run on your micro. But beware! As often happens to programs that have existed in the public domain for any appreciable length of time, there are many noncompatible versions of X-modem. For best results, check with people that are using the version that you have obtained to ensure that it actually works with your particular application.

These important concepts summarize the material in Chapter 5:

- The ultimate dot-matrix character appears to be continuous, not actually a product of a finite number of dots.
- Each dot-matrix character on a video display resides in an imaginary character box.
- A CRT is constructed from an electron gun, horizontal and vertical deflection coils, and a phosphor-coated screen.
- The horizontal sync signal blanks the electron gun and returns the beam to the beginning of the next line.
- The vertical sync signal blanks the electron gun and returns the beam to the first line of the display.
- Typical character attributes are: blinking, underlined, reverse video, and intensified.
- A character-generator ROM contains the dot patterns of the 96 printable ASCII characters.
- Characters are painted on a video display in a row-by-row process.
- A typical RS-232 terminal contains a logic board, monitor board, power supply, CRT, and detachable keyboard.
- ROMs that contain programs are called firmware.
- Most microcomputers employ a video display that contains only a monitor board, power supply, and CRT. The equivalent of the terminal's logic board is contained in the microcomputer's enclosure.

- Bit-mapped graphics do not use a character generator but illuminate the screen on a dot-by-dot basis.

- Typical terminal setup parameters are: communications baud rate, printer port baud rate, number of data bits, number of stop bits, local or duplex operation, full- or half-duplex, character or block mode, parity enable, type of parity, emulation mode, normal or reverse video, refresh rate, CR only or CR/LF, and monitor-mode enable.

- Terminal setup is accomplished by positioning DIP switches on the rear of the terminal or via the keyboard with a built-in setup program.

- Typical communications baud rates for direct connect terminals are 4800, 9600, and 19,200.

- The printer port on terminals is a DCE port. This enables printers (DTEs) to be directly connected to the terminal.

- Most mini- and mainframe computers employ 7 data bits per character.

- The only devices that require more than 1 stop bit are electromechanical tele-types and similar equipment.

- In local mode characters are not sent to the UART.

- In full-duplex mode characters are transmitted by the UART but not to the video display. It is expected that the remote computer will echo the character.

- In half-duplex each character is transmitted by the UART and also sent to the video display. It is assumed that the remote computer does not have the ability to echo characters.

- In block mode characters are simply sent to the video display. When the send key is depressed, all the characters on the video display will be transmitted by the UART.

- In character mode each character is transmitted as it is entered on the key-board.

- Many terminals have the ability to emulate popular terminals. This is impor-tant if a particular terminal is not supported on a computer system but the user wants to run a full-screen application that requires cursor addressing.

- The refresh rate of terminals used in the United States and Canada is the same as the power line frequency, 60 Hz.

- When computers append an LF to each CR, the terminal should be set to CR only.

- Monitor mode enables the terminal to display the 32 control characters. In this manner terminal driver software can be debugged.

- Terminals have two levels of self-tests. The first type displays the entire char-acter set on the video display. The second type employs a loop-back plug to verify the operation of the RS-232 interface.

- A driver is a low-level program that acts as a translator for hardware-dependent functions.

- Computer systems must have a terminal driver for each type of supported terminal.
- There are many print modes supported on terminals.
- The break key does not send an ASCII character. It transmits a long interval-spacing level. It is pressed when a terminal is completely locked up and needs to be reset by the computer.
- Microcomputer communications programs provide three services: communications, terminal emulation, and file transfer.
- A dumb terminal does not support cursor addressing or other advanced features.
- Most communications programs support an emulation mode, where the microcomputer appears as a popular type of terminal.
- Transferring a file from a large computer to a micro is called down-loading.
- Transferring a file from a micro to a large computer is called up-loading.
- Files can be transferred using simple data capture. However, this method does not guarantee the integrity of the data.
- Asynchronous communications protocols are used to ensure that ASCII files and binary files are transferred without error.
- Computers can transfer files via an asynchronous RS-232 interface only if they both support the same file-transfer protocol.
- Kermit and X-Modem are two popular file-transfer protocols used with micros.

6

Modems, Printers, and Print Buffers

In this chapter we examine the operation and setup considerations of modems, printers, and print buffers. These devices are among the most popular RS-232 peripherals. On completion of this chapter you will have sufficient knowledge to understand the documentation, setup parameters, and interface considerations of any RS-232 device.

6.1 MODEM PROTOCOLS

Modems are classified by *standard protocols* that define the baud rate, method of modulation, and specific manner in which logic levels are represented. Two modems are compatible only if they both employ the same protocol. Modems that support multiple protocols automatically configure themselves to the protocol of the modem that originates the conversation. Do not confuse modem protocols with communication protocols such as Kermit.

The *Bell-103* protocol (the oldest modem standard in common usage) defines a 300-baud modem that employs *frequency modulation* (FM) to convert signals between the digital and analog worlds. Within frequency modulation, the logic 0 and logic 1 levels are represented as different frequencies.

How is full-duplex communication accomplished between modems? A user initiates a conversation by employing a modem and terminal to dial up a remote computer. The local modem is described as the *originator* and the remote modem functions in the *auto-answer mode*. The Bell-103 protocol defines the two frequencies at which the originator transmits logic levels and two additional frequencies at which the answering modem transmits logic levels. Simply put, the transmit frequencies of the originating modem correspond to the receive frequencies of the answering modem. The same relationship is true for the transmit frequencies of the answering modem and the receive frequencies of the originating modem. In this manner four audible frequencies are employed to implement simultaneous data transmission between a terminal and computer via the standard public switched telephone network.

Most newer modems have the capacity to function in originate and answer modes. Obviously, most users employ their modems only in originate mode—when would a typical microcomputer user employ a modem in the auto-answer mode? In the last chapter we discussed terminal emulation and file transfer. When two microcomputer users need to establish communications, one modem operates in originate mode (as normal) and the other must perform in the auto-answer mode. After the connection is established, programs and data can be transferred between the micros using Kermit, X-MODEM, or other file-transfer protocol.

Most popular asynchronous modems communicate at 1200-baud and employ the *Bell-212A* or *Racal-Vadic* protocol. These modems utilize *phase modulation* (PM), in which the phase of the carrier is varied instead of the frequency (as in the Bell-103 protocol). The major difference between the Bell-212A and Racal-Vadic protocols is the frequency of the carrier. This means that not all 1200-baud modems are compatible. To overcome this obstacle many answer-only modems connected to the communications ports of mini- and mainframe computers support both the Bell-212A and Racal-Vadic protocols. In addition those special modems also often support the Bell-103 protocol. A user with any of these three types of modems can dial up an electronic *bulletin board service* (BBS) or large computer, and the answering modem will automatically configure to the protocol of the originating modem.

Three hundred-baud modems are painfully slow and can actually incur greater operating expenses than 1200-baud modems. Consider the implications of a lengthy file-transfer operation between computers that are thousands of miles apart. At 300 baud, the time required to transfer the file is appreciably longer than at 1200 baud. The extra charges for computer-connect time, long-distance phone connection, and personnel expenses are a strong argument in favor of the superior performance of faster modems.

6.2 MODEM INDICATORS

Let's examine the typical indicators that are featured on 1200-baud modems. These modems are physically packaged in a small rectangular box with the bulky power supply transformer at the end of the power cord. Figure 6.1 illustrates the typical front-panel indicators found on 1200-baud modems. These indicators provide status information regarding data flow, hardware handshaking, and remote-carrier status.

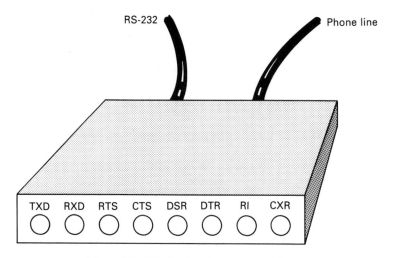

Figure 6.1   1200-baud modem front panel indicators.

Because the carrier detect line on the RS-232 interface is known by many different names (DCD, CD, RLSD), abbreviations such as CXR are employed to label the data carrier detect indicator. This indicator illuminates to signal that the modem has sensed the carrier of a remote modem. Modems that support 300- and 1200-baud communications usually have a *high-speed* (HS) LED that illuminates to indicate 1200-baud operation.

The modem is connected to the serial port of the terminal or microcomputer through a standard RS-232 cable with pins 1–8 and 20. Older modems have a two-position *voice/data switch*. In the voice position, the telephone handset sharing the phone line with the modem can be used for normal voice communications. To establish a remote connection, the user manually dials the phone number and, when the user hears the high-pitched sound of the remote modem's carrier, the user toggles the switch into the data position. This action causes the local modem to output its originate carrier, and the connection is established.

6.3 SMART MODEMS

Newer modems are called *smart modems*. As we have seen "smart" indicates that a device has local, on-board intelligence, usually in the form of a microprocessor and firmware. Commands to smart modems are issued by a communications program (running on a micro) or from the keyboard of a terminal or micro. The most useful of these commands is *auto-dial*. Instead of dialing the remote modem manually with an external handset and waiting for the carrier tone to flip a voice/data switch, the user of a smart modem commands the modem to dial the number. A telephone handset is no longer required to be connected to each modem line. Many modems have a memory of 10 to 20 phone numbers, which are stored in battery-backed

RAM. The appropriate command lists the phone numbers in the modem's directory, and a number can be selected and auto-dialed.

There are many utility programs that support auto-dial modems for microcomputers. These programs provide the services of creating, sorting, and searching phone directories stored on a floppy or hard disk. The computer can be employed as an automatic dialer for normal voice communications.

Hayes Microcomputer Products, Inc., developed a smart modem with a sophisticated instruction set. *Hayes standard* instructions are supported by most of the popular communications programs and auto-dial utilities. Microcomputer users are well advised to purchase modems that guarantee to be *Hayes compatible*. Like the RS-232 hardware interface standard, which creates a hardware-independent environment at the physical interface, the Hayes standard creates a software-independent environment between a communications program and the smart modem. By no means is the Hayes standard the only supported application-to-modem instruction set, but it is the most popular and boasts the largest installed base. If you already own a non-Hayes compatible modem, before you purchase communications software check with the manufacturer or vendor to ensure that your particular modem is supported.

6.4 STAND-ALONE AND INTERNAL MODEMS

Microcomputer modems are available in *stand-alone* and *internal* versions. Stand-alone modems can be used with RS-232 terminals and microcomputers that have an RS-232 port. Internal modems are implemented on a single *printed circuit board* (PCB) and are designed to function with specific microcomputers. They plug into the expansion slots or I/O connectors on the system board of the microcomputer. Let's consider the advantages of internal and stand-alone modems.

Advantages of a stand-alone modem

1. Hardware independent: functions with any RS-232 terminal or microcomputer with RS-232 port.
2. Usually has many indicators (as illustrated in Figure 6.1) that assist the user in troubleshooting malfunctioning systems connections.
3. Can easily be transported and checked on another terminal or microcomputer.
4. Does not take up an expansion slot on the system board of a microcomputer.

Advantages of an internal modem

1. Does not increase the *footprint* of a microcomputer system. The footprint of a computer refers to the amount of desk space a unit occupies.
2. Usually 15% to 25% less expensive than stand-alone modems.

3. Does not require an external RS-232 port on microcomputer. (The port is contained on the modem board.)

4. Usually has an on-board speaker that enables the user to hear the modem dial and establish connection.

5. No external RS-232 cable or AC outlet is required.

In large computer facilities where many banks of modems are used to handle the huge volume of dial-up lines, *rack-mount* modems are often employed. Rackmount modems are stand-alone modems that are mounted in electronic equipment racks. These racks supply the DC voltages required by the modems.

6.5 MODEM SETUP

Modem setup varies from the trivial to the complex. There are two major concerns while interfacing a smart modem to a terminal or microcomputer. Most modems are disabled until they sense an active level on DTR. If your terminal or microcomputer communications program does not automatically assert DTR, then the modem must be instructed to be enabled at all times and ignore the state of DTR. This is accomplished with a jumper or DIP switch on the modem.

Another common setup problem concerns the DCD line. Remember that the receiver portion of many UARTs is not enabled until an active level appears on DCD. The user and smart modem must communicate prior to the connection with a remote modem. Commands entered by the user or issued by the communications program should be echoed to the video display by the modem; additionally, the modem will send status information detailing the process of dialing the number and the condition of the remote connection—busy, no answer, 1200-baud connection, and so on. If the UART needs to see an asserted DCD line, then commands will not be echoed, nor will the status information be displayed. Like the DTR setup just discussed, modems provide a jumper or DIP switch to assert DCD permanently to ensure that the receiver of the local UART is always enabled.

Many modems are also capable of performing several types of self-tests. The *digital loop-back* test checks the digital portion of the modem. *Analog loop-back* verifies both the digital and analog portions of the modem. If the self-tests pass and the modem still malfunctions, the manufacturer can dial up the suspect modem and run *remote diagnostics*.

Many modems do not have a standard 25-pin RS-232 D-type connector. Their interface cable must be ordered directly from the manufacturer. One end of this cable has a custom connector designed for the specific modem and the other end has a standard 25-pin male or female connector that plugs into the RS-232 port on the terminal or micro.

The latest generation of asynchronous modems communicates at 2400 baud. At the time of this writing there are no recognized standard communications or hardware error-checking and retransmission protocols. There is no doubt that a standard will soon emerge, and prices of 2400-baud modems will quickly fall. Within a short period 1200-baud modems will be displaced by the new generation of 2400-baud modems.

6.6 DOT-MATRIX AND DAISY-WHEEL PRINTERS

Traditionally, printers have employed an RS-232 port to interface with computers and terminals. With the advent of the IBM-PC the *Centronics parallel interface standard* has become the most popular method of connecting microcomputers to printers. Parallel interfaces do not serialize data but instead transmit an ASCII character in one simple operation employing eight data lines and several handshaking and status lines. Figure 6.2 illustrates the parallel interface.

Because the ASCII character is sent in a single operation instead of a bit stream, the overhead associated with the serial interface is not applicable to the parallel interface. The user need not be concerned about baud rate, number of data bits, number of stop bits, and type of parity. The parallel interface operates at TTL voltages. This limits the length of the interface cable, constructed from shielded cable and twisted pair conductors, to under 30 feet.

There are still many applications that require the use of serial interfaces on printers. In this section we overview the major types of printers and the typical setup options associated with serial printers.

Until recently, the major types of printers were *dot-matrix* and *daisy-wheel*. The *print head* of a dot-matrix printer consists of a vertical column of pins (typically seven). The dot-matrix character is printed in a column-by-column operation. This

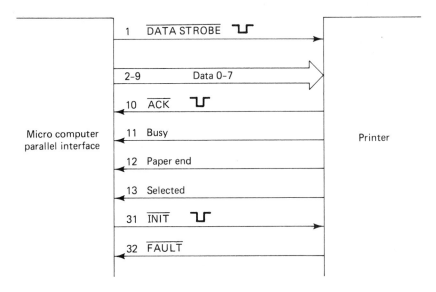

Figure 6.2   Microcomputer/printer parallel interface.

is the opposite of the way in which characters are created on video displays. At printing speeds up to 200 characters per second (cps), dot-matrix printers are considered relatively fast. But the quality of documents produced by these printers does not meet the high standards demanded in office environments. Dot-matrix printers can be programmed to operate in near-letter-quality (NLQ) mode, but this cuts the normal print speed by 50% to 75% due to the fact that each column is printed twice, with a slight offset to enhance the dot-matrix character. A dot-matrix printer that prints 160 cps in normal mode typically prints 40 to 60 cps in NLQ mode. Even though NLQ is a great improvement over draft quality, it is still unacceptable in most offices.

A new generation of 24-pin print-head dot-matrix printers can produce acceptable letter-quality documents at extremely high speeds. Although they are still two to three times as expensive as 7-pin printers, these new 24-pin printers will quickly fall in price and become extremely competitive.

Earlier we saw how video displays can operate in an APA (all-points-addressable) bit-mapped mode. Dot-matrix printers with graphic options can also operate in a bit-mapped manner. The process of character creation on video displays and dot-matrix printers is exceedingly similar. In normal operation the equivalent of the character-generator ROM (that we studied in video displays) takes the ASCII character as it is received by the printer's interface circuitry and creates the column dot patterns to represent the character. In graphics mode printers do not employ a character-generator ROM but essentially work in an APA mode. Thus complex graphics created on CRTs can be printed by extremely inexpensive dot-matrix printers. This is an outstanding feature of dot-matrix printers that should not be undervalued.

As a logical extension of this graphics capability, dot-matrix printers can be programmed to print in many foreign and scientific language sets and *character fonts*—from the Greek alphabet to elegant calligraphy. We know that computers must have a driver program for each terminal type that they suppport. Similarly, custom drivers must be written to exploit the infinite number of character sets, fonts, and special effects (underlining, bold, superscripts, subscripts, and so on) that dot-matrix printers support. These drivers are provided with word-processing programs and also marketed as utility software packages.

Daisy-wheel printers produce letter-quality documents. This type of printer is named from the circular print wheel, typically constructed from 96 spokes. At the end of each spoke is an embossed character. The print wheel is said to resemble the daisy flower with its many petals. The daisy-wheel is rotated until the appropriate character is in place; the character is then struck by a hammer mechanism against an ink ribbon and paper. The rotation process severely restricts the performance of daisy-wheel printers. But because the character is continuous, the high quality and readability of documents produced by daisy-wheel printers make them necessary in office environments. Daisy-wheel printers can print only the set of 96 characters that are embossed on the daisy-wheel in current use. Daisy-wheels must be changed to create different character sets or font sizes.

Daisy-wheel printers are much more expensive than comparable dot-matrix printers. Furthermore, most require the additional options of a *tractor feed* and *acoustical enclosure*. The tractor feed is driven off the *platen* (paper roller) gear and pulls the pin feed paper and multipart forms through the paper path. Dot-matrix and daisy-wheel printers emit a loud and annoying noise at a level intolerable in most offices. The printer must be placed in an acoustical enclosure, which reduces the sound to a bearable level. Tractor feeds and acoustical enclosures are expensive add-ons, which should be considered prior to purchasing a daisy-wheel printer.

Also of concern in offices is the printing of documents on company letterhead. This letterhead can be specially ordered (at a premium) on continuous feed paper. An alternative is to purchase a *single-sheet feeder*. Single-sheet feeders are mechanical devices that are similar to tractor feeds. Many sheets of letterhead are placed into the single sheet feeder in much the same way that paper is placed into a photocopy machine. At the reception of each FF character, a new sheet is fed into the platen roller mechanism. Single-sheet feeders, tractor feeds, and acoustical enclosures must be ordered for each particular printer—one size does not fit all.

To summarize, we list the advantages of dot-matrix and daisy-wheel printers.

Advantages of dot-matrix printers

1. Inexpensive.
2. Fast in draft mode.
3. Capable of graphics printing, different language sets, and different fonts.

Advantages of daisy-wheel printers

1. True letter quality.

The top of the printer market has traditionally been dominated by daisy-wheel printers. That market is now in the process of being invaded by nonimpact printers, the most popular of which is the *laser printer*. Laser printers look like personal-sized photocopy machines. Because they print (like photocopy machines) by the page instead of the line, the speed of laser printers is rated in *pages per minute* (ppm). Laser printers operate very quietly and reliably. Hewlett-Packard has set the standard for the low-cost laser printer market with the HP Laser-Jet printer. The Laser-Jet prints 8 ppm with a high resolution of print density at 300 dots per inch (dpi).

Laser printers are capable of producing near *camera-ready-* or *type-set-* quality documents with integrated text and graphics. They have enabled small companies to create their own in-house publishing departments. No longer do documents have to be sent out for the time-consuming and expensive process of typesetting.

Because of the high performance, quality, and reliability of laser printers, they will soon dominate the high end of the letter-quality printer market. Daisy-wheel printers will battle 24-pin dot-matrix printers as a midcost alternative to inexpensive dot-matrix printers and high-performance laser printers.

Another type of nonimpact printer is the *ink-jet printer,* which creates a dot-matrix character by shooting charged droplets of ink at a special type of paper. Ink-jet printers are extremely quiet (as are all nonimpact printers) and very fast. The least expensive of the ink-jet printers are successfully competing in the dot-matrix printer market.

All these printers are available with either parallel or serial interfaces. Serial interfaces are selected for environments where the printer may be connected to an RS-232 terminal, microcomputer, or computer network.

6.7 SPECIAL EFFECTS

All printers are capable of producing the standard printable ASCII characters from 20H to 7FH. Daisy-wheel printers simply rotate the appropriate spoke into position, where it is stuck by the print hammer. Dot-matrix printers (which include normal dot-matrix, laser, and ink-jet printers) employ a character-generator ROM to create the dot patterns of the printable ASCII characters. Daisy-wheel and dot-matrix printers are also capable of special effects such as underlining, bold print, super-scripts, and subscripts. Furthermore, we have already noted that dot-matrix printers can also produce different character sets and font sizes.

As is true with terminals, each make and model of printer employs a unique set of control codes and escape sequences to invoke the special print attributes. Let's take a moment to understand how these special effects are integrated into standard documents. Imagine that you are using a popular word-processing program designed to run on a specific microcomputer. The computer keyboard and perhaps a mouse are the input devices. The video display and printer are the output devices. The document is created and edited on the video display. When you are satisfied with the appearance of the document on the video display, you send it to the printer.

Word-processing programs have a setup mode where operational parameters are selected. One of the important parameters is to choose the model of printer that will be used as the hard-copy output device. The word-processing program installs the appropriate printer driver to translate the special effects as they are displayed on the video display into the specific control codes and escape sequences required to drive the printer.

Figure 6.3 is a listing and output of a program written in BASIC. This program demonstrates the control codes and escape sequences that are employed by the IBM-PC Graphics Printer. An LPRINT command prints the information in quotes directly to the printer. Thus LPRINT ''A'' sends an ASCII 41H to the printer. Usually a <CR>/<LF> sequence is appended to the end of each LPRINT command line. The example LPRINT ''A'' actually sends the three characters ''A''(41H), CR(0DH), and LF(0AH) to the printer. If the argument of an LPRINT statement is

```
10 REM *** Program to display typical dot matrix printer attributes ***
15 REM The following control codes are used in decimal by the program
20 REM ESC = 27, SO = 14, S1 = 15, DC2 = 18, DC4 = 20
25 REM Each control code or escape sequence is shown on individual lines
30 LPRINT "Draft Quality - High Speed"
35 LPRINT CHR$(27);"E";
40 LPRINT "NLQ (Near Letter Quality) at half speed";
45 LPRINT CHR$(27);"F"
50 LPRINT CHR$(27);"G";
55 LPRINT "Bold print at one quarter speed";
60 LPRINT CHR$(27);"H"
65 LPRINT CHR$(27);"-";"1";
70 LPRINT "Underlined print mode";
75 LPRINT CHR$(27);"-";"0"
80 LPRINT CHR$(14);
85 LPRINT "Double width print";
90 LPRINT CHR$(20)
100 LPRINT CHR$(15);
105 LPRINT "Compressed print @ 136 characters/line";
110 LPRINT CHR$(18)
115 LPRINT "Subscript H";
120 LPRINT CHR$(27);"S";"1";
125 LPRINT "2";
130 LPRINT CHR$(27);"T";
135 LPRINT "O"
140 LPRINT "Superscript e = mc";
145 LPRINT CHR$(27);"S";"0";
150 LPRINT "2";
155 LPRINT CHR$(27);"T"
```

```
Draft Quality - High Speed
NLQ (Near Letter Quality) at half speed
Bold print at one quarter speed
Underlined print mode
Double  width  print
Compressed print @ 136 characters/line
Subscript H₂O
Superscript e = mc²
```

Figure 6.3 BASIC program listing and output.

followed by a comma or semicolon, the <CR>/<LF> is suppressed. With those facts in mind let's examine lines 100 through 130 in the program listing.

Line 100.   This line is a REMark that indicates that the lines following demonstrate the way in which the underline attribute on the IBM-PC graphics printer is invoked and terminated.

Line 110.   The BASIC command CHR$() is used to send control codes and escape sequences to the printer to display. (Note that the argument for CHR$() is assumed to be a decimal number.) Thus LPRINT CHR$(27) sends the ESC character to the printer. This tells the printer to interpret the next printable ASCII character(s) as part of a command sequence. The ESC , - , 1 sequence causes all subsequent characters to be underlined.

Line 120. The string constant "Underlined print mode" will be underlined.

Line 130. This line sends the ESC , -, 0 command string to the printer, which terminates underlined print mode.

The actual printer drivers employed by word-processing programs are usually written in the assembly language of the computer's native processor. This program was intended to offer a simplified example of printer-control codes and escape sequences. Notice that once a printer is instructed to operate in a particular print mode, it will do so until the appropriate terminate command is issued, or it is reset by turning off the power, or a system software-reset operation occurs. Thus it is a fairly straightforward process to write BASIC programs to invoke useful print modes. As an example, assume that you are using a spreadsheet program and want to print a full-size 132-column page on a standard carriage width (80 columns) dot-matrix printer. The BASIC program that sets the printer to condensed print mode can be executed before you enter the spreadsheet program. On exiting the spreadsheet, you could run a BASIC program that terminates the condensed print mode or simply toggle the printer's power switch on and off.

6.8 SETUP PARAMETERS OF SERIAL PRINTERS

The setup operation of serial printers is accomplished by setting DIP switches and jumpers. The setup for baud rate, parity enable, and parity type function are exactly like their terminal counterparts. Instead of the CR/CR-LF parameters that we saw with terminals, printers require a choice of CR or LF as the *end-of-block* (EOB) character; CR is usually selected.

Some printers support many different serial printer-communications protocols. The great majority of the time, either hardware handshaking via DTR or software handshaking with X-ON/X-OFF is selected. Other applications are rare, and you must consult your computer documentation to establish the exact manner in which printer data is transmitted.

Printers have a *first-in, first-out* (FIFO) buffer memory, which is typically 256 bytes to 2K bytes. Figure 6.4 illustrates the relationship of the buffer memory and the print mechanism. Buffer memory is fast and can easily keep up with a computer sending data at 19,200 baud. The problem is that the buffer memory quickly fills and, unless the computer is informed of this condition, the buffer will overrun and characters will be lost. As we have already discussed, RS-232 devices can handshake by means of software or hardware.

Software handshaking or flow control is accomplished by the X-ON/X-OFF protocol. When the buffer reaches a set capacity, the printer transmits an X-OFF

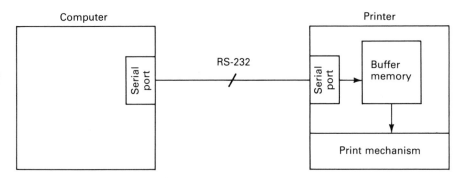

Figure 6.4   Buffer memory in a printer.

character. If the printer driver supports X-ON/X-OFF flow control, the computer ceases data transmission and enters an idle mode. After the buffer empties to a particular level, the printer transmits an X-ON character, and the computer resumes data transmission. When people think of a computer sending data to a printer, they usually do not consider the fact that the printer may be sending flow-control characters back to the computer. Remember that if X-ON/X-OFF flow control is selected, the printer cable must have transmit-data (pin 2) and receive-data (pin 3) lines. Do not assume that all printer drivers support flow control—the IBM-PC's RS-232 communications *basic input/output system* (BIOS) does not support X-ON/X-OFF handshaking.

The levels at which the buffer-full (X-OFF) and buffer-empty (X-ON) codes are sent can be selected. The setting that you choose depends on the maximum size block of data that will be sent by the computer. Most printers buffer data until a CR/LF sequence is received. Most computer systems have a maximum line buffer length of 256 bytes. That is, there will never be more than 256 characters between CR/LFs. Assuming this to be the case, if a particular printer has a 2K buffer memory, then it should send X-OFF when the buffer has 256 free bytes of storage remaining and X-ON when the buffer has emptied to less than 256 characters.

If the printer waits to send an X-OFF character until only 128 bytes are left, the character may arrive too late, just as the computer is starting the transmission of a 256-byte block of data. The buffer may be overrun, and consequently data could be lost. Block sizes other than 256 bytes are rare. Just remember that an X-OFF character must be sent when there is enough room left in the buffer for one block of data.

What happens if a printer driver does not support flow control protocol? Printers (just like terminals) are classified as DTEs. Hardware handshaking in printers is often called *printer-ready* protocol. When the buffer is approaching a full condition, the printer usually brings DTR (pin 20) to an inactive marking level. This causes the computer to cease data transmission. When the buffer has emptied to the appropriate level, the printer asserts DTR to a spacing level, and the computer resumes data transmission.

To complicate this otherwise-simple handshaking process, printers may utilize pin 11 of the RS-232 interface as an alternative printer-ready line. Often part of the setup of the serial interface boards on printers is to choose whether pin 20 or pin 11 is used for hardware handshaking. In Chapter 8 we consider the entire setup operation of the serial interface illustrated in Appendix A.

The third way for printers and computers to handshake is not to handshake. Handshaking is required only to stop data transmission when the printer's buffer is about to overflow. If the baud rate is set low enough so that the printer can actually keep pace with the data flow, then no handshaking need take place. Usually we want to optimize computer efficiency by setting the highest possible baud rate between the computer and printer and utilizing some form of handshaking to avoid buffer overflow.

Certain printers simultaneously support a serial and a parallel interface. One of the setup parameters is to select which interface is currently active. Other printers have a physical location for both types of interfaces, but they cannot be concurrently installed. Be sure to check your manufacturer's documentation regarding these points.

How do printers handle parity errors? Most printers and terminals print the @ character in place of any character received with a parity error. We discuss troubleshooting printer connections in Chapter 8.

All printers have extensive firmware-based (ROM) self-tests. These self-tests can be directed to print out the entire character set of the printer. This verifies the entire printer operation with the exception of the serial interface. To validate the operation of the interface, a *loop-back plug* (illustrated in Figure 5.6) is placed onto the RS-232 connector of the printer. The printer sends print data out of its TD pin, and the loop-back plug has a jumper that steers the data back into the RD pin of the printer. The DTR output is looped back to the DSR input. This tests for proper hardware handshaking. The loop-back test verifies the operation of the RS-232 interface.

6.9 SOFTWARE-BASED AND STAND-ALONE PRINT BUFFERS

Most microcomputers are described as *single tasking*, which means that they can perform only one job at a time. When a word-processing program is sending a document to a printer, the computer cannot be used to perform other tasks until the print operation is complete. This is often an appreciable length of time.

There are two methods of resolving this printer bottleneck. One is to employ *print-buffer software* that makes a microcomputer appear to be *multitasking*. A print-buffer program reserves a specified amount of system RAM. When the word-processor program is instructed to output a document to the printer, the print-buffer program intercepts the system print call and redirects the data into the RAM buffer. This is an extremely fast operation. It appears to the word-processor program that the print operation is complete and the user can then reenter the word processor to edit other documents, or a new applications program can be loaded from disk and executed.

How does the print data stored in the RAM buffer get sent to the printer? Computers have hardware timers that are programmed to interrupt the system processor each time a specific period has elapsed. This interval is usually 25 to 50 ms. The computer uses this interrupt to update the system's *time-of-day* (TOD) clock and other time-dependent *housekeeping* functions. The print-buffer program "intercepts" this timer interrupt and sends the printer a block of data from the RAM buffer. This operation only takes a few milliseconds, and then the print-buffer program returns system control to the timer-interrupt routine.

Notice that this process makes extremely efficient use of computer time. The sluggish aspect of printer operation (from the computer's point of view) is waiting for the buffer to empty before sending the next block of data. By employing the print-buffer program, the computer is allowed to carry out standard processing during the period when it would normally be waiting for the printer's buffer to empty. Print-buffer programs are fairly simple, and many exist in the public domain. See your local users' group for a listing of free print-buffer programs.

For computers that do not support software print buffers and also for use with printers that are connected to the auxiliary port of RS-232 terminals, a hardware solution must be invoked to resolve the printer bottleneck. Figure 6.5 depicts the relationship of the *stand-alone print buffer* to the computer and printer or terminal and printer. Stand-alone print buffers have two RS-232 connectors—one for the connection to the data source (microcomputer or aux port of a terminal) and another to be connected to the RS-232 interface of the printer. Typical print buffers contain

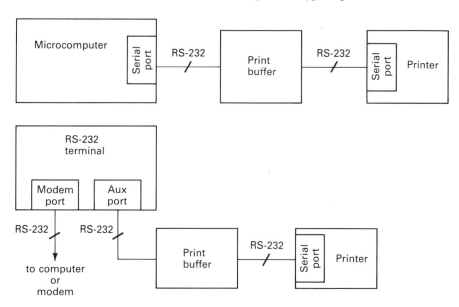

Figure 6.5   Stand-alone print buffer.

64K bytes to 256K bytes of RAM. This RAM provides the same function as the RAM buffer in the microcomputer's software print buffer; it can also be considered as an extension of the RAM buffer on the serial interface of the printer.

The print buffer contains a microprocessor that controls the stream of print data, flow-control handshaking, and hardware handshaking. To understand fully the operation of the print buffer, we must consider two cases.

Case 1: *The print data fits into the RAM on the print buffer.* The entire file of print data is sent to the print buffer. Because the print buffer's RAM will not overflow, the transfer occurs quickly, with no delays. It is the responsibility of the print buffer to handshake with the printer. Print buffers support X-ON/X-OFF flow control and DTR printer-ready handshaking. The printer cannot differentiate between receiving data directly from the computer or via the print buffer.

Case 2: *The print data does not completely fit into the RAM on the print buffer.* The computer sends data until the RAM on the print buffer is nearly full. The print buffer then sends an X-OFF character or drops DTR to signal that data transmission must be suspended. When the buffer RAM is nearly empty, the print buffer transmits an X-ON character or asserts DTR and the computer resumes sending data. While the first RS-232 interface of the print buffer is receiving print data and handshaking with the computer, the other RS-232 interface of the print buffer is transmitting data and handshaking with the printer.

The print buffer should be transparent to the print operation; it should look like a printer to the computer and like a computer to the printer. The amount of RAM in the print buffer should be larger than the largest document that you will normally print. This enables the computer to dump all its print data to the print buffer without any delays. The print buffer then performs the routine process of handshaking with the printer.

The setup of print buffers occurs in two phases. The first step is to configure the front end of the print buffer to match the requirements of the computer in terms of baud rates, parity, number of data bits, type of handshaking, and so on. The RS-232 port that connects with the terminal or computer is a DTE interface— remember that the print buffer must look like a printer to the computer. The second step is to perform the same setup for the printer side of the print buffer. This RS-232 port is a DCE connection, which makes the printer appear to be connected to a computer or modem.

Print buffers offer a feature that enables the user to obtain multiple copies of a document. The data stored in the buffer is simply held and reprinted the required number of times. Other options enable the print buffer continually to store data sent by the computer but not print it until explicitly instructed. This feature is valuable with print buffers that are connected to terminals. The printer port of the terminal can remain enabled, but the user selects which data is actually printed.

Many print buffers support *split baud rate* operation. This enables the computer and printer to operate at different baud rates, further increasing the efficiency of the print operation by letting the computer send data at a faster baud rate than may be supported by the printer.

Print buffers are available that also perform *interface conversion*. These devices can connect computers with serial printer interfaces to parallel printers and parallel computer ports to serial printers.

These important concepts summarize the material in Chapter 6:

- Modems are classified by protocols.
- The Bell-103 protocol defines a 300-baud modem that employs FM.
- The Bell-212A and Racal-Vadic protocols define a 1200-baud modem that employs PM.
- The modem that initiates the conversation is called the originator.
- The extra overhead associated with file transfer makes faster modems less expensive to use.
- Modems have many indicators that display the status of the RS-232 handshaking lines.
- Older modems have a voice/data switch that is used manually to enable the carrier of the modem.
- Smart modems have an on-board microprocessor. They are capable of executing instructions sent from the keyboard of the terminal or a communications program.
- Smart modems are often used with utility programs to create auto-dialers on microcomputer systems.
- The Hayes standard defines a set of modem instructions that are supported by popular micro communications programs.
- Stand-alone modems can be used with any RS-232 port.
- Internal modems are designed to be used with a specific microcomputer.
- Modems often have to sense an active level on DTR before they will accept instructions from the terminal or micro.
- Many UARTs must see an active level on DCD before the transmitter is enabled. Because the micro or terminal must communicate with a smart modem prior to establishing a remote connection, the DCD output of the modem may need to be jumpered to an active level.
- Many modems do not have a standard RS-232 connector.
- The Centronics parallel interface standard is the most popular way to connect printers to micros.
- Dot-matrix and daisy-wheel printers dominate the micro printer market.
- Dot-matrix printers can be programmed to output foreign language and scientific character sets and many print fonts.
- Daisy-wheel printers produce letter-quality documents.
- Typical options with daisy-wheel printers are acoustical enclosures, tractor feeds, and single-sheet feeders.

- The new generation of nonimpact printers is based on the laser printer.
- Laser printers produce high-resolution near type-set-quality documents at extremely high speeds.
- The ink-jet is another popular form of nonimpact printer that competes in the dot-matrix printer market.
- Serial interfaces are selected for printers that must be used with a wide variety of computers and terminals.
- Typical printer special effects are underlining, bold print, superscripts, and subscripts.
- Applications programs typically supply drivers for dozens of the most popular printers. This ensures that the user will be able to use all of the printer's special effects.
- A printer indicates a full buffer by sending an X-OFF character or by disasserting DTR.
- Not all printer drivers may be assumed to support X-ON/X-OFF flow control.
- Printers may hardware handshake on DTR or pin 11.
- If a computer and printer cannot handshake properly, the baud rate should be slowed down to the point where the printer can actually keep up with the data flow.
- Most printers have firmware-based self-tests.
- Software print buffers allocate a certain amount of RAM in a microcomputer as a temporary storage area for print data.
- Software print buffers are programs that are specific to each type of microcomputer. They can be obtained from the public domain.
- Stand-alone print buffers essentially expand the amount of storage in the printer's buffer.
- Stand-alone print buffers are designed to handshake with both the data source and the printer.

7

Designing and Constructing RS-232 Interface Cables

There are many different configurations of cables used to interface RS-232 devices. Each cable consists of two connectors and the insulated wires that run between them. The type of connectors and wires that are used in RS-232 cables is dependent on the length of the cable, cost considerations, and the availability of special tools used to crimp pins on the wires. In this chapter we discuss cable design, construction methods, and, most importantly, empirical design techniques.

7.1 DTE-TO-DCE INTERFACE CABLE

We know that asynchronous RS-232 devices use pins 1 through 8 and 20; we have also noted that pin 11 is used in some printer handshaking operations, and pin 22 represents the ring-indicator signal, which may be infrequently required. Some interface cables have as few as 3 wires. Others provide all 25 wires, even though most will be unused.

Think back to one of the first concepts that you learned about RS-232. The DTE transmits data on pin 2 and outputs handshaking-status information on RTS and DTR. The DCE transmits data on pin 3 and outputs handshaking-status information on CTS, DSR, and DCD. Figure 7.1 illustrates the simple cable that is used to interface a terminal (DTE) to a modem (DCE).

Notice that pin 1 of the terminal is connected to pin 1 of the modem. This one-to-one correspondence applies to every wire in a DTE-to-DCE cable; because

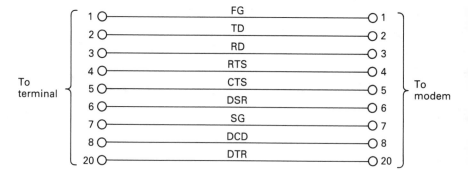

Figure 7.1 Modem cable—pins 1–8 and 20—straight through.

the cable is symmetrical, either end can be connected to the DTE or DCE. You will discover that this relationship is not true for all RS-232 cables. If all 25 pins are connected straight across, the pins not employed by the asynchronous interface are simply ignored.

What is the least number of wires that must be run in a DTE-to-DCE cable? That depends on the requirements of the specific DTE and DCE. Most terminals (DTEs) do not implement a rigorous interpretation of the RS-232 handshaking signals; they usually ignore CTS, DCD, and DSR. Modems, on the other hand, usually do implement strict handshaking procedures: RTS must be active to enable the transmitter in the UART of a modem, and DTR must be active to enable the receiver in the UART of the modem. When in doubt, connect all lines 1 through 8 and 20.

7.2 DTE-TO-DTE INTERFACE CABLES

DCEs exist solely to support long-distance communications between DTEs. It makes perfect sense that DTEs are often directly connected without intervening modems. Remember that the RS-232 interface is designed to connect DTEs to DCEs. The straight-through cable used to connect a terminal to a modem will not work to connect a terminal directly to a computer.

A special cable must be utilized to connect DTEs directly. This cable is called a *modem-eliminator, null-modem* or *crossover* cable. The function of this cable is to deceive each DTE into "thinking" that it is connected to a modem.

Figure 7.2(a) is a table that groups the inputs, outputs, and grounds of the RS-232 interface as referenced to the DTE. With the aid of this table, we can apply the concept of the loop-back test plug from Chapter 5 to create a modem-eliminator cable. Although both FG and SG are illustrated in Figure 7.2.(b), frame ground is not always implemented. The transmission of data is handled quite simply: TD from one DTE drives the RD input of the other DTE.

There is one awkward point in the one-to-one relationship between inputs and outputs of the RS-232 interface. TD is coupled with RD and RTS is associated with

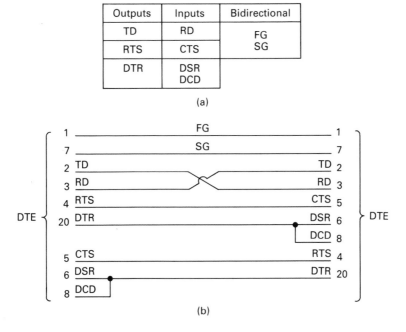

(a)

(b)

Figure 7.2   RS-232 signals grouped by function.

CTS. But DTR relates to both DSR and DCD. A modem must indicate not only its own on-line status (by DSR) but also the status of a connection to a remote modem (by DCD). We have seen that some UARTs require an active level on DCD to enable their receivers; yet other UARTs may only scan for an active level on DSR.

When constructing a modem-eliminator cable, it is always prudent to tie DSR and DCD together. This guarantees that whatever modem handshaking line the local UART or software driver happens to be monitoring, will be correctly driven by DTR on the remote end of the connection. As was mentioned in the previous paragraph, relate the pinout of the loop-back test plug in Figure 5.6 to the modem-eliminator cable in Figure 7.2(b).

Let's consider the modem-eliminator cable illustrated in Figure 7.3. There are only three wires in the cable. The function of frame ground is to guarantee that dangerous volts do not exit between the frames of the two devices connected by the cable. In the majority of cases frame ground and signal ground are tied together on the circuit board containing the RS-232 interface circuitry. Additionally frame ground and signal ground are usually connected to earth ground via a three-prong power plug. This implies that if both devices on the interface are connected to earth ground, then SG doesn't have to be run on the interface cable. That may be true in many cases, nevertheless, it is wise to run a signal ground on all RS-232 cables; consider frame ground as an option for equipment that is not connected to earth ground via a three-prong power plug.

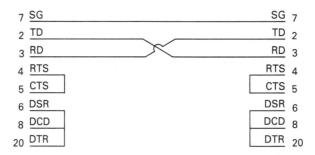

Figure 7.3 Minimum wire modem-eliminator cable.

The other two lines in the cable are TD and RD. All the handshaking lines are looped back in the fashion of the loop-back test plug.

A major limitation of the cable in Figure 7.3 is that hardware handshaking is not supported! All handshaking must be accomplished by X-ON/X-OFF flow control. As we have discussed, most RS-232 devices support flow control. If the cable in Figure 7.3 is to be used, remember to select X-ON/X-OFF protocol on the setup of both devices connected by the interface cable.

Another limitation of the cable in Figure 7.3 is the lack of a DTR signal to indicate when a device is powered up and ready to receive data. Consider a printer that is connected to a microcomputer via an RS-232 port. How will the computer actually know that it is sending data to a "live" (powered-up and on-line) printer? We have seen that an active level on DTR or pin 11 of the RS-232 interface is used as a printer-ready signal. Figure 7.4 illustrates an improved version of the cable in Figure 7.3. This cable, unlike the others that we have examined, is not symmetrical—each end must be connected to the appropriate device. On the computer side of the interface, we see that DSR and DCD are driven by the printer-ready signal. This signal is at an active spacing level when the printer is powered up, on-line, and does not have a buffer-full condition. The rest of the handshaking sig-

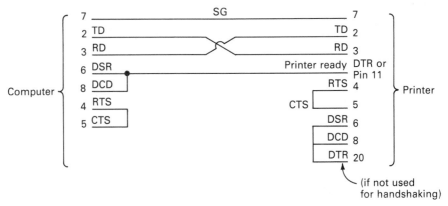

Figure 7.4 Printer interface cable with printer-ready signal.

nals are looped back. Because both TD and RD lines are run, the computer and printer have the option of employing X-ON/X-OFF flow control or printer ready. If a computer does not support X-ON/X/OFF flow control, then the TD data line from the printer need not be run. Nevertheless it is good practice to include this line—cables should be designed to operate in the most general application.

Many printers do not require CTS, DSR, or DCD to be at active levels. It is still a good practice to loop these signals back. The rule of thumb is to loop back those handshake signals that are not used in the data exchange or handshaking process.

7.3 THE BREAK-OUT BOX

At this point you should be able to consult the manufacturer's documents on any two RS-232 devices and perform the internal setup and design of an interface cable. In reality, that is a best-case scenario; operator's manuals are (more often than not) inadequate and teeming with errors, and you are often expected to interface a microcomputer to a printer without the aid of any documentation.

For the remainder of the book, we use the example of interfacing a microcomputer to a printer. This is one of the most common and least understood RS-232 interfacing operations.

Let's make a short list of some common questions that must be answered before the interface cable can be designed:

Microcomputer

1. What handshaking signals must the UART (or printer driver) see to enable its receiver? Transmitter?
2. Does the microcomputer support hardware or software (X-ON/X-OFF) handshaking?
3. How are the baud rate, number of data bits, number of stop bits, and parity enable/type set?

Printer

1. What handshaking signals must the UART see to enable its receiver? Transmitter?
2. Does the printer support hardware or software (X-ON/X-OFF) handshaking?
3. What pin does it use for printer ready: pin 20 or pin 11?
4. How are the baud rate, number of data bits, number of stop bits, parity enable/type, and buffer control parameters set?

Some printers have the setup information for the RS-232 interface written on the back panel or inside the case. Sometimes the setup cannot be accomplished without the manufacturer's documents. The setup of RS-232 ports in microcomputers is usually accomplished in the applications software (communications program, word processor, spreadsheet, and so on) or by executing the appropriate operating system command.

In this section we examine a device that will enable us empirically to design RS-232 interface cables. "Empirical" means "by inspection"—relying on experience or observation alone. The empirical method substitutes test equipment in place of manufacturer's documentation. For RS-232 interface cable design, this test equipment often takes the form of the inexpensive, yet extremely powerful and flexible, *break-out box* (BOB).

An RS-232 break-out box consists of 24 switches and jumper/patch points, 10 to 14 LED indicators, a package of assorted test jumpers, and two short lengths of interface cable terminated in standard DB-25 connectors. Some break-out boxes have DB-25 connectors attached directly to the sides of the boxes and supply a short

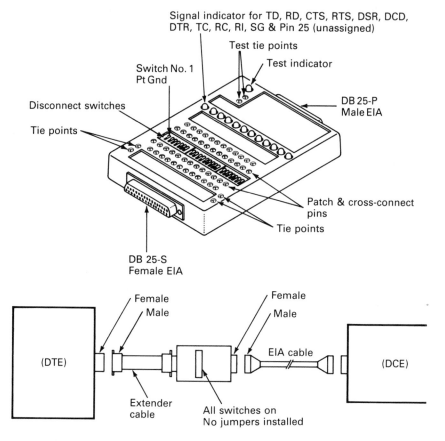

Figure 7.5   Typical break-out box and connection in the interface cable.

length of interface cable with a female and male connector on each end. Figure 7.5 is a drawing of a typical break-out box (BOB).

BOBs use LEDs to monitor the logic state of the important data and handshaking lines of the RS-232 interface. Simple BOBs use a single LED for each line. This LED illuminates to indicate a spacing level. When the LED is not illuminated, the line is at a marking (-3 V to -12 V) or indeterminate level ($+3$ V to -3 V). To alleviate this ambiguity between marking and indeterminate levels, newer BOBs employ two LEDs or a tri-state LED for each line.

Accepting the universal interpretation that green indicates ''go'' and red indicates ''stop,'' on a dual-LED BOB a green LED illuminates to indicate a spacing level and a red LED illuminates to signify a marking level. If neither LED is illuminated, the line is in an indeterminate state. Tri-state LEDs contain a green and red LED within a common enclosure. They function in an identical manner to the dual LEDs.

Some BOBs use batteries to power their LED indicators. The LEDs in newer BOBs are powered from the line in which they are monitoring. Line-powered BOBs require that the RS-232 driver supply 3 mA to 5 mA of current in addition to the current requirements of the RS-232 receiver in the remote equipment. Although this extra current draw is usually of little significance, it is an important fact that should be duly noted.

Figure 7.6 illustrates the model of each line in the BOB that is monitored by a dual or tri-state LED. The BOB is inserted in the interconnection cable between the two serial devices. When the switch on a particular line is closed, the BOB appears transparent and the signal propagates as normal. The voltage drop of the tri-state LED plus a standard silicon diode is approximately 3 V. This ensures that only a legitimate mark or space will illuminate the LED indicator. Notice that there is a

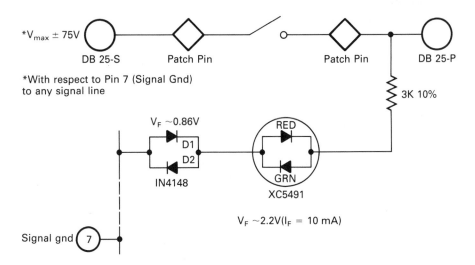

Figure 7.6   Model of one line in a break-out box.

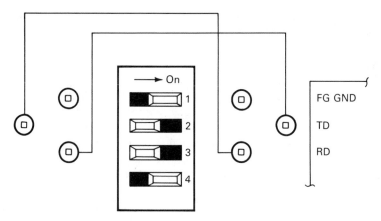

Figure 7.7 Cross-patching TD and RD.

patch pin on each side of the switch. This enables signals to be cross-jumpered, as in Figure 7.7.

To help you appreciate the versatility of the BOB, let's create the equivalent of a loop-back plug. Figure 7.8 illustrates the pertinent lines of a break-out configured to function as a loop-back plug. Assume that you have inserted a BOB between a microcomputer and a modem. You invoke a communications program and enter terminal emulation mode. When a command is sent to the modem, nothing is echoed to the video monitor of the micro. This may be due to a malfunction or incorrect setup of the modem, or the microcomputer may not be functioning as an RS-232 terminal because of an incorrect setup, malfunctioning communications program, or a hardware failure of the RS-232 interface circuitry in the microcomputer.

You should always check the obvious first: Is the power switch of the modem turned on? Is it plugged into a working AC outlet? Are the RS-232 connectors snug on both ends of the connection?

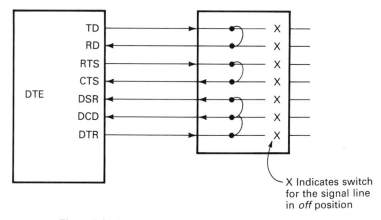

Figure 7.8 Break-out box configured as a loop-back plug.

   The next possibility to consider is whether the microcomputer is functioning
as a terminal. The switches of the lines that the modem is driving must be opened at
the BOB: RD, CTS, DSR, and DCD. Using the jumpers supplied with the BOB,
TD is patched to RD, RTS is patched to CTS, and DTR is patched to DSR and
DCD. Jumper wires are provided that *patch* (jumper) two points together or *daisy
chain* many points together. The BOB is now functioning as a loop-back plug. All
keystrokes should appear on the video display.

   This test only indicates that the microcomputer is acting like a terminal. It
says nothing about the baud rate or other setup factors that could be the cause of the
malfunction. We investigate troubleshooting techniques and procedures in great detail in Chapter 8. This illustration is designed to indicate how easily the BOB can be
used to modify the interface.

   It is important to ensure that output drivers are never jumpered together. As
you may remember from Chapter 3, the RS-232 standard guarantees that output
drivers must be designed to withstand short circuits to any voltage between + 25 V
and − 25 V. In the next chapter we investigate what happens when drivers are
shorted together. For now, just accept the fact that this operation will result in un-
known voltage levels and should not damage the RS-232 equipment or BOB.

   As another exercise in using BOBs to modify an interface, let's create the
modem-eliminator cable illustrated in Figure 7.2. Figure 7.9 illustrates a BOB
configured as a modem-eliminator cable. All the switches are opened except for SG.
(Some BOBs internally jumper around the switch that controls SG to prevent the
loss of a ground reference.) As we have discussed, if SG is tied to earth ground and
both devices on the interface are connected to AC power via a three-prong plug,
then the interface should function without a signal ground. Never assume this to be
true; always connect SG between the two units on the interface cable!

   DCD and DSR are jumpered on each side of the interface. The rest of the
outputs are jumpered to the appropriate receivers on each side of the interface. Fig-

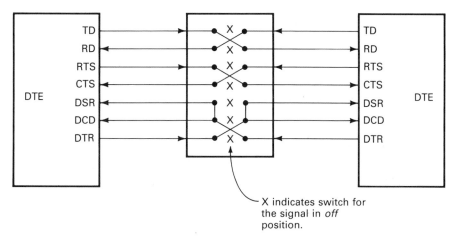

X indicates switch for
the signal in *off*
position.

Figure 7.9 Break-out box configured as modem-eliminator cable.

ure 7.9 distinctly illustrates why modem-eliminator cables are often called crossover cables.

The following features should be considered when purchasing a BOB:

1. Is it battery or line powered?
2. What type of indicators does it employ: single LED, dual LED, or tri-state LED?
3. Does it include a reasonable number of double, triple, and quadruple patch jumpers?
4. Are universal gender connectors provided? This means that a male and female connector are provided for each side of the interface. This is a great convenience factor.
5. Does it include a protective and practical carrying case?

7.4 USING THE BOB TO DESIGN PRINTER INTERFACE CABLES

Let's use the BOB to design a cable that connects a microcomputer to a printer. Assume that we have all the information required to set up the microcomputer for the correct baud rate, number of data bits, and so on. But we do not have any information describing the implementation of signals on the RS-232 interface or the type of handshaking used by either device.

Printers are classified as DTEs. They always receive data on pin 3 and transmit data on pin 2. Recall that the printer port on a terminal is configured as a DCE. The serial port on a microcomputer may be configured as a DTE or a DCE. Some micros have a general-purpose RS-232 interface that is intended as a port to connect modems, printers, or any other RS-232 device. These general-purpose ports are always configured as DTEs. Modems are connected to such ports with straight-through cables, whereas printers require modem-eliminator cables. When a micro has two built-in RS-232 ports, one is configured as a DTE (to be connected to a modem) and the other is configured as a DCE (to be connected directly to a printer.)

How do we empirically establish whether an RS-232 port is a DTE or DCE? Consider two cases, the first with a single-LED BOB and the second with a dual-LED or tri-state LED BOB.

Case 1: *The marking level on TD does not illuminate the TD indicator.* A DTE often brings RTS and DTR to an active level on power up. If either of these LEDs is illuminated, the port is a DTE. A DCE brings DSR active level on power up. If the DSR LED is illuminated, the port is a DCE. A voltmeter can be employed to measure the voltage between TD and SG and RD and SG. The line on which data is transmitted should be at approximately -12 V DC.

Case 2: *The marking level on data output of the RS-232 device causes the TD or RD LED on the BOB to glow red* (refer to Figure 7.10), *thus identifying the type of interface.* This is a situation that proves how valuable it is to be able to monitor

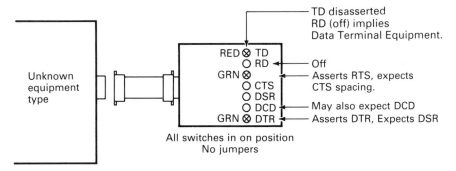

Figure 7.10   Using a tri-state LED break-out box to establish equipment type.

both inactive marking levels and active spacing levels. Also note which handshaking lines are driven and their particular logic levels. This tells you how the device appears on power up and what handshaking signals it asserts.

If the microcomputer port is a DCE, the connection to the printer is implemented via a straight-through cable. A DTE port requires a modem-eliminator cable.

Now we must establish whether the printer utilizes X-ON/X-OFF flow control or hardware handshaking. There are many ways to establish this important parameter. We are going to try the most intuitive method. If we are interfacing the printer to a DCE port, we simply connect the two devices together via the BOB and a straight-through cable. If the computer has a DTE port, configure the BOB as a modem-eliminator cable as illustrated in Figure 7.4. Assume, for the moment, that the printer uses DTR as the printer-ready signal.

We now want to have the microcomputer send a file large enough to fill the buffer of the printer and cause the printer to disassert printer ready or send an X-OFF character. The time interval required to fill the print buffer depends on the baud rate of the connection and the size of the printer's buffer. There are five likely events that may occur when the print buffer fills:

1. The LED on the BOB that is monitoring DTR of the printer (and DSR and DCD of the microcomputer) changes to a marking level (glows red), and the TD LED goes to a marking level (also glows red) to indicate that the microcomputer has temporarily suspended data transmission. After a short interval, the printer takes printer ready (DTR) to an active level (glows green), and the microcomputer resumes sending data (indicated by a flickering TD LED.) This process repeats until the print operation is complete.

2. The LED on the BOB that is monitoring DTR of the printer does not go to an inactive marking level, but the TD goes to an inactive marking level, indicating the suspension of data transmission. This implies that the printer is using X-ON/X-OFF protocol. After a brief period, the print buffer empties and the printer transmits an X-ON character. The print operation then continues.

3. DSR and DCD on the microcomputer side of the interface never goes to an active spacing level because the printer is hardware handshaking on pin 11 instead of pin 20. Most BOBs do not monitor pin 11 with an LED. Move the jumper from DTR on the printer side of the interface to pin 11 on the printer side of the interface. Toggle the power on the printer (to clear the buffer-full condition), and the DSR and DCD LEDs on the microcomputer side of the interface should now indicate an active level. The printer operation should then proceed as illustrated in Case 1, with pin 11 substituted for DTR on the printer side of the interface.

4. If the print operation appears normal for a short period but then the printer starts dropping characters and printing *garbage*, the print buffer has overflowed due to a failure in handshaking between the printer and microcomputer. If DTR or pin 11 on the printer side of the interface never went to an inactive marking level, this indicates that the printer is probably using X-ON/X-OFF handshaking, and the printer driver employed by the microcomputer does not support flow-control handshaking. The setup of the printer must be changed to select printer-ready hardware handshaking.

5. The printer does not print—absolutely nothing happens! This is often the case. The next chapter is devoted to troubleshooting. We discuss the steps required to verify the operation of the microcomputer, printer, and the communications cable.

The order of the day when empirically designing cables with a BOB is "roll up your sleeves and experiment." Take confidence in the RS-232 specification that guarantees that output drivers can withstand a short circuit to any wire on the interface. Simply put, you probably won't hurt anything. Be bold and adventurous. You understand how the interface *should* function; experiment to see how it *actually* functions. When the interface is working properly, take a moment to document clearly and concisely everything that you have discovered. This simple precaution eliminates the need to "reinvent the wheel" for similar connections.

7.5 REALIZING THE PHYSICAL INTERFACE

You have learned how to employ a BOB empirically to design an interface cable. But it is much too expensive to dedicate a BOB to every cable; how do we transform the interface cable created with the BOB into a permanent cable? In this section we consider the different types of wire, connectors, pins, and interfacing paraphernalia commonly used to create interface cables.

Our first concern is to establish the *gender* of connectors that will be used on each end of the cable. *Female connectors* employ *sockets* and *male connectors* employ *pins*. A DB-25P designates a male RS-232 connector and DB-25S designates a female RS-232 connector. The RS-232 specification states that the female connector should be associated with the DCE. This implies that each end of the interface cable will have different gender connectors. But because it is as common to connect DTEs together as it is to connect a DTE to a DCE, the RS-232 specification concerning the genders of connectors is completely ignored by the industry.

Most terminals have two female connectors, one for the modem port and another for the printer port. In opposition to the industry norm, Digital Electronics Corporation (DEC) places male connectors on its terminals.

The same confusion is also true in the microcomputer world. Most RS-232 ports on micros have female connectors, with the notable exception of the IBM-PC, which employs male connectors on its RS-232 asynchronous communications adapter.

Most people prefer to have female connectors on the equipment and male connectors on the cables. The logic for this choice is simple yet compelling: The pins that constitute male connectors are easily bent and broken. It is better to break the pin on a cable that is easily replaced than the pin on the connector soldered to an interface board, whose repair often requires extensive disassembling, desoldering, and special parts.

Establish the types of connectors associated with each device to be joined by the interface cable. The opposite-gender connector is assigned to the associated end of the cable. For example: The cable required to connect a female connector on a terminal to a female connector on a modem requires a male connector on each end.

If a cable is nonsymmetrical and both connectors are the same gender, care must be taken to label each connector clearly and permanently. It is extremely frustrating trying to establish if the malfunction of a computer/printer connection is due to a transposed cable.

Now that we have established the gender of the connectors, the type of wire used in the cable must be selected. Let's examine the most popular forms of wire used to construct RS-232 interface cables.

Ribbon cable.   *Ribbon cable* is a flat cable with small-diameter stranded wires molded together in a horizontal plane. For RS-232 applications, ribbon cables are ordered with 25 wires. Ribbon cable with more than 25 wires can easily be trimmed down by slicing off the extra connectors with a razor-knife.

Insulation displacement connectors are used with ribbon cable. These connectors have a slotted metal finger for each wire. The ribbon cable is fed into a slot on the back of the insulation displacement connector. The first wire in a ribbon cable (colored red or blue) should be aligned with the pin-1 (an arrow) indicator on the connector. The connector is then placed into a vise or similar mechanism, where each metal finger in the connector is driven into the appropriate wire. The connector derives its name from the action of the metal fingers piercing through the insulation and securing contact with the conductor.

On your first few cables, the ribbon cable may be slid to one side of the connector, resulting in a misalignment of pin 1. Also pay close attention and match the pin-1 indicator (arrow) on the connector with the colored wire on the cable. Be patient, and with a little practice you will find that constructing cables with ribbon cable and insulation displacement connectors is an extremely quick and easy process. Figure 7.11 illustrates a section of ribbon cable and an insulation displacement connector.

Ribbon cables suffer from two major limitations. First, they have considerable amounts of capacitance, which places severe limits on their maximum lengths. The maximum length of a cable must be established empirically because it is dependent on the baud rate that it supports. The author's experience indicates that the practical length of a ribbon cable supporting 9600-baud communications is 150 ft. For cables over 10 ft long, ribbon cable is usually not the best solution.

The other limitation of ribbon cables involves connecting DTEs to DTEs. It is not practical to create a modem-eliminator cable with ribbon cable. The conductors run straight through and cannot be crossed over and slipped through the connector without great effort.

A device created to solve this problem is illustrated in Figure 7.12. The plastic cover on this device lifts off to reveal that the seven signals of interest in an RS-232 asynchronous interface are terminated at solder pads. The modem-eliminator cable designed with the aid of the manufacturer's documents or a BOB can be constructed by soldering jumpers between the appropriate pads. The in-line jumper adapter can be thought of as an extension of a ribbon cable and can be used to create custom modem-eliminator cables with a minimum of tools and time. The in-line jumper adapter is usually placed on the connector of one of the devices in the interface. The

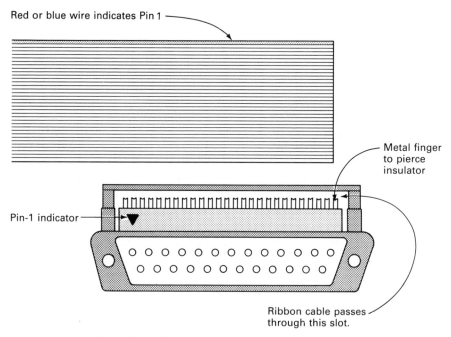

Figure 7.11   Ribbon cable and insulation displacement connector.

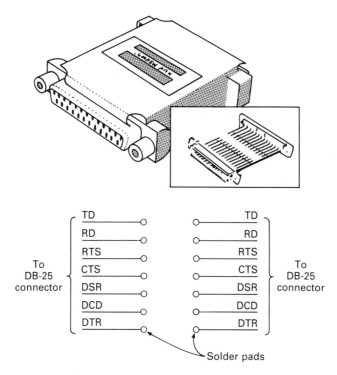

Figure 7.12   RS-232 in-line jumper adapter.

interconnection cable is then plugged into the second connector on the in-line jumper adapter.

Transmitting AC signals through unshielded wires results in the radiation of stray electric fields. These fields cause *crosstalk* in parallel wires (as in ribbon cable). A method of combating this problem is to twist adjacent wires. This effectively cancels stray electric fields.

Twisted-pair multiconductor wire is constructed from pairs of twisted, insulated wires housed within an outer jacket. Each wire is color coded. Twisted-pair wire can be purchased with 1 to 50 pairs within the outer jacket. When a full RS-232 cable is constructed, 12-pair wire is used. For most asynchronous applications, 2- to 4-pair wire is sufficient.

The outstanding characteristic of ribbon cable is the ease with which insulation displacement connectors are installed. The use of twisted-pair cable requires that each wire be stripped of approximately ¼ in. of insulation and that a pin (for male connectors) or socket (for female connectors) be placed on the end of each wire. One type of pin and socket is designed to be squeezed onto the wire with a *crimping tool*. Inexpensive crimping tools can be difficult to use and may yield questionable contacts. Good crimping tools are moderately expensive and should be purchased only if you plan on manufacturing a reasonable number of cables.

After the pins or sockets are crimped onto the ends of the wires, they must be inserted into the male or female DB-25 *shell*. A *pin insertion/extraction tool* is used to insert and remove wires from the connector. This tool is useful for modifying cables to fit new needs.

An alternative to crimp-type pins and sockets is the *solder-type* connection. Instead of using a crimping tool to squeeze the pin onto a wire, the stripped portion of the wire is inserted into the pin or socket and soldered. This guarantees a solid connection, but it is not as quick or easy as a crimping operation.

Shielded cable.   The conductors in *shielded cable* are housed within an aluminum mylar shield. This shield protects the wires within the cable from radio-frequency interference that may induce data errors.

Long-distance cable.   Remember that the maximum length of a cable is inversely proportionate to the capacitance of the wire and the baud rate. *Long-distance cables* are optimized for low capacitance, which increases their maximum length without the use of active components such as amplifiers and filters.

Materials that you use to construct cables are often those that are convenient or already at hand. Both ribbon cable and twisted pair (using crimp-on or solder pins and sockets) make good cables. Factors to consider are the length of the cable and whether you want to incur the added expense of using an in-line jumper adapter with ribbon cables to construct modem eliminator cables.

7.6 RS-232 UTILITY DEVICES

Many computer-supply companies feature devices that are designed to facilitate the connection and enhance the performance of RS-232 devices. In this section we examine a few of the many items that are available.

Devices called *line drivers* are used to double or triple the maximum length of an RS-232 cable. These external line drivers should not be confused with the line-driver ICs found on serial interfaces.

The most inexpensive line drivers are inserted halfway along the interconnect cable. They act as ''repeaters'' by amplifying and filtering the data and handshaking signals. Because line drivers are amplifiers, they have active components and must be plugged into AC outlets.

A more expensive type of line driver that greatly extends the maximum length of a cable is purchased in pairs. Each line driver is connected to the terminating RS-232 device with a short cable. The two line drivers are then connected via a long length of two-pair twisted-pair cable.

These line drivers function in a similar fashion to modems. When a signal is referenced to a common ground, that signal is described as *single-ended*. Sophisticated line drivers employ *differential* signals. A separate ground is run for TD and RD. A *differential amplifier* is used to recover the difference between TD and RD and their associated grounds. Any noise induced in the long RS-232 line has an equal amplitude in both the transmit signal and its ground. The differential amplifier recovers the original signal by amplifying the difference between TD and its ground and RD and its associated ground.

The voltage levels that exist between the two-drive drivers are not RS-232 compatible. Thus the line drivers amplify and transform each signal on the RS-232 interface. As stated previously, line drivers are similar to modems, but instead of employing audible tones to transmit data, they use *double-ended*, or differential, signals. Notice that only TD and RD are sent between the line drivers. The line driver monitors the DTR line on its local RS-232 device and generates a pseudo-DTR signal to indicate to the remote line driver that a device is powered up and on-line.

RS-232 line and modem spike protectors.   Most microcomputer users are aware that high-voltage transients generated by the *inductive kick* of electromechanical devices (refrigerators, photocopy machines, electrical element heaters, and so on) can cause premature aging or failure of an electronic system. AC line-surge protectors are employed to protect computers and printers. Surge protectors clip and filter transients before they reach the AC inputs of power supplies.

Close-proximity lightning strikes can induce high-voltage surges into phone lines and RS-232 cables that are strung through the air and along buildings. Surge protectors are available to protect the internal circuitry of modems and RS-232 drivers and receivers. In areas such as the Midwest, where lightning strikes are common, these surge protectors can save considerable time and money.

Gender changers.   How do you resolve the conflict that occurs when the connector on a cable and the connector on the RS-232 device are the same gender? Instead of changing the gender on a functioning cable, a gender changer can be applied. A gender changer is simply a small module constructed from back-to-back connectors of the same gender. As an example, to connect the male connector of a cable to a male connector on a serial interface, a gender changer consisting of back-to-back female connectors is employed. Gender changers constructed from back-to-back male connectors are used to facilitate the connection of a female cable connector to a female serial interface connector.

Gender-independent cable.   The *gender-independent cable* is a short ribbon cable with female and male connectors on each end. It functions as both a female-to-female and a male-to-male gender changer. A gender-independent cable is especially helpful when used with a BOB.

RS-232 switches.   Many times a computer that has only one RS-232 port must be time-shared between two devices, such as a modem and a printer. Instead of manually changing the interface cable of the selected device into the serial port of

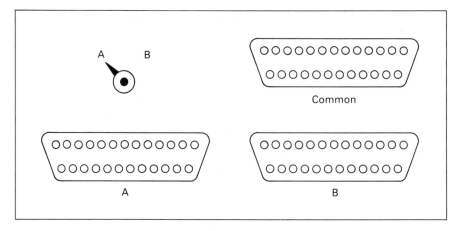

Figure 7.13 RS-232 switchbox.

the computer, an RS-232 switchbox can be used. Figure 7.13 illustrates the typical layout of such a box. The RS-232 port of the computer is connected to the *common input* connector. The peripherals are fastened to connectors A and B. The two-position switch controls which peripheral is electrically connected to the RS-232 port of the computer.

It is often desirable to connect a terminal directly to a local computer and also have a modem to access remote computers. The RS-232 switchbox is perfect for such an application. Consider the situation where a small office with two microcomputers purchases a high-performance laser printer. Both computers must be able to use the printer. The printer can be connected to the common connector on the switchbox with the two micros connected to the A and B connectors.

RS-232 switchboxes are available with up to four inputs switchable to one common output. If your printer handshakes on pin 11, be sure that the manufacturer of the particular switchbox runs this line. Many manufacturers run only lines 1 through 8 and 20.

These important concepts summarize the material in Chapter 7:

- DTE-to-DCE cables usually have a one-to-one correspondence between each pin in the RS-232 interface.
- The straight-through cable used to connect a DTE to a DCE will not work to connect DTEs directly.
- A modem-eliminator cable is used to connect a DTE to a DTE.
- When constructing modem-eliminator cables, it is wise to jumper DSR and DCD together.
- A minimum wire DTE-to-DTE cable runs SG, TD, RD lines. It is assumed that X-ON/X-OFF flow control will be employed.

- It is important to run a line for pin-7 SG on every RS-232 interface cable.
- Cables constructed to connect the DTE port of a microcomputer to a printer will not be symmetrical. Each end must be properly labeled.
- A cable that supports both X-ON/X-OFF flow control and printer ready/busy handshaking must include RD and DTR lines.
- The break-out box is used as an aid to empirically design cables and troubleshoot interfaces.
- Dual LED or tri-state LED BOBs indicate both valid marking and spacing levels.
- Line-powered BOBs are convenient because one need not worry about dead batteries.
- When a BOB is used to interface a DTE to a DTE, all switches except SG should be opened.
- Unless labeled differently, serial ports on microcomputers are configured as a DTE.
- The type of interface port (DTE or DCE) can be discovered by establishing what data line and handshaking lines are driven.
- A red LED indicates a marking level, and a green LED indicates a spacing level.
- To establish empirically the type of handshaking employed by a printer, a buffer-full situation should be forced while monitoring the handshaking with a BOB.
- If a printer prints correctly for a few pages and then starts outputting garbage, this indicates that the buffer has overflowed due to a failure in handshaking.
- After the successful testing of a new interface cable, take a moment to document the design and other relevant information.
- Ribbon cable is used with insulation-displacement connectors.
- The maximum length of an RS-232 cable constructed from ribbon cable is greatly limited due to an excessive amount of capacitance.
- In-line jumpers are used to create modem-eliminator cables with ribbon cables.
- In twisted-pair cables, two wires are twisted together to minimize crosstalk.
- Crimp- or solder-type pins are used with twisted-pair cable.
- Insertion/extraction tools are used to install pins in connectors and modify interface cables.
- Shielded cable has an aluminum shield to protect the enclosed wires from radio-frequency interference.
- Long-distance cables are optimized for low capacitance.
- External line drivers are used to increase the maximum length of an interface cable.

- High-performance line drivers employ differential transmitters/receivers.
- RS-232 line and modem spike protectors are used to guard against damage caused by lightning strikes.
- Gender changers enable two connectors of the same gender to be joined.
- A gender-independent cable has both a female and a male connector on each end.
- RS-232 switches allow two or more RS-232 devices to share the same port.

8

Troubleshooting Interface Malfunctions

In the last chapter we learned how to empirically design, construct, and test interface cables. In this chapter we consider what actions should be considered when two devices are connected (by what is construed to be the correct cable) but do not function at all or in an incorrect manner.

We first examine the process of installing a serial port in an IBM-PC and installing and setting up a serial port in an Okidata-92 dot-matrix printer. In the later part of the chapter we consider troubleshooting interfaces with the BOB (break-out box), DMM (digital multimeter), and oscilloscope.

8.1 INSTALLING A SERIAL PORT IN AN IBM-PC

Because you are known as the resident RS-232 expert, a small department in your company has requested your assistance in setting up a microcomputer and serial printer. They have ordered an IBM-PC with the optional asynchronous communications adapter, Okidata-92 dot-matrix printer, the optional serial interface board for the printer, and a standard modem-eliminator cable.

The installation procedure of the asynchronous serial adapter in the IBM-PC is well documented. But there are a few odd characteristics of the serial port on the IBM-PC that must be considered. First, unlike most serial ports on DTE, the DB-25 connector on the IBM-PC is male. This indicates that we may need a gender changer because the interface cable was probably ordered with male connectors on each end.

We must remember that the IBM-PC's BIOS driver does not support X-ON/ X-OFF protocol. Handshaking must be accomplished through hardware. According to the BIOS listing found in the IBM *Technical Reference Manual*, the PC will assert DTR and RTS, and the driver program checks for active levels on DSR and CTS before communications can commence. This fulfills the typical hardware handshaking that we have described throughout the book.

It should be noted that the UART used on the asynchronous communications adapter on the PC (INS8250) does not have specific handshaking requirements set in hardware. It is entirely up to the driver program to control and interpret the handshaking lines. Many applications programs available for the IBM-PC replace the BIOS async driver with their own custom drivers, in which they may interpret the handshaking lines in a different manner. It is safe to assume that the driver will assert DTR and CTS, and we will ensure that CTS, DSR, and DCD are taken to active levels to enable the UART.

One final word of caution about the IBM-PC's async card lies in the type of RS-232 line receivers it employs. Instead of using the industry standard 1489 (as described in Chapter 4), IBM employs the 75154 with the compensation inputs tied to $+5$ V. The relevant difference between these receivers is the way in which they interpret an open circuit input.

Consider the case where the interface cable between a computer and printer is loose or has fallen off: The inputs of CTS, DSR, and DCD are not being driven; they are said to be *floating*. It is extremely important that a receiver interpret a floating input as a marking (off) condition. In this way a computer will not send data to a printer that is turned off or whose interface cable has fallen out. This is such an important specification that it is explicitly stated in paragraph 2.5 of the EIA RS-232C Standard.

Each of the four line receivers in the 75154 has a *threshold input*. This input is used to provide noise immunity by modifying the characteristic response of the receiver. In formal electronics terminology, the modified response curve is called a *hysteresis loop*. The threshold inputs of the line receivers in the PC's async card are tied to $+5$ V. This results in an interesting input characteristic.

Let's assume that the DSR input is greater than $+3$ V, a valid spacing level. The DSR input must go more negative than -3 V before the receiver interprets the input as a marking level. Simply put, the 75154 receiver with threshold input tied to $+5$ V will not fulfill the RS-232 specification of interpreting a floating input as a marking level! It essentially *latches* (remembers) the last valid RS-232 level. This provides a noise immunity of 6 V because a minimum of 6 V of noise must be riding on a valid RS-232 level before the output is pulled in the opposite direction.

This hysteresis characteristic can result in a few odd and apparently intermittent problems. The critical question is: On power up, how does the 75154 line receiver interpret the floating CTS, DSR, and DCD inputs? The answer is randomly. This means that an incorrectly constructed interface cable may work half the time! This is a problem that the author has seen numerous times.

The IBM-PC can support two RS-232 ports, which are designated as COM1: and COM2:, where COM stands for communications port. The position of an 8-pin header that plugs into an IC socket on the interface board determines the designation of a particular async adapter. The asynchronous communications adapter is inserted into any empty slot in the PC bus.

IBM provides a standard diagnostic diskette with each PC system unit. The diagnostic program should be executed after the asynchronous communications adapter is installed. That will ensure that the microprocessor in the PC can communicate with the UART on the async port.

An Advanced Diagnostic Diskette is available from IBM. Its powerful features include a loop-back test for the serial ports. This test verifies that the UART, line drivers, and line receivers are functioning correctly.

8.2 THE INSTALLATION AND SETUP OF A SERIAL PORT IN A DOT-MATRIX PRINTER

Assuming that the async adapter has been correctly installed and tested, we now turn our attention to the installation and setup of a serial interface board in a dot-matrix printer.

Appendix A is the user's manual for the serial interface board of the Okidata-92 dot-matrix printer. This particular serial board was selected because it has all the features found in most simple serial interfaces and also boasts many sophisticated functions.

Read Appendix A to enhance and test your knowledge of RS-232 interfaces. Most of the concepts should be familiar. The following paragraphs discuss specific parts of the user's documentation.

Pages 151 through 153 illustrate how to install the serial board into a printer equipped with the standard parallel printer interface. Note that Step 10 indicates that the function switches on the interface board must be set before operation is attempted. These switches define the printer's communications specifications, handshaking, and protocol.

Step 11 indicates a task that is often forgotten. After the serial board is installed, the printer has two interfaces—parallel and serial. One of the function switches is used to activate the serial interface and thus deactivate the parallel interface.

Page 135 describes the printer-interface requirements. It states that the cable connector attached to the printer must have a DB-25P connector, where P stands for "plug," or male connector. It also sets the maximum length of the interface cable at 50 ft of shielded, twisted-pair cable. This is an extremely conservative estimate based on the assumption of printer operation at 9600 baud. For most applications this length can be doubled or tripled without inducing errors.

Let's examine the description of the RS-232 interface signals on pages 138 and 139, as reproduced in Figure 8.1.

RS232C SERIAL INTERFACE SIGNALS

Pin No.	Signal	Direction	Description
1	Protective ground (PG)	—	Connected to printer frame (frame ground)
2	Transmitted data (TD)	From printer	Serial data signal transmitted from printer
3	Received data (RD)	To printer	Serial data signal received by printer
4	Request to send (RTS)	From printer	Transmission request signal from printer. SPACE during transmission.
5	Clear to send (CTS)	To printer	Reply signal to RTS signal. Printer transmits data after confirming this signal as SPACE.
6	Data set ready (DSR)	To printer	Signal to notify printer that transmitter is ready for transmission. Printer receives data after confirming this signal as SPACE.
7	Signal ground (SG)	—	Signal ground
8	Carrier detect (CD)	To printer	For MODEM connection only: this signal is connected to the modem CD signal. Printer receives data after confirming this signal as SPACE.
11 or * 20	Supervisory send data (SSD)	From printer	Signal to indicate that the printer is not ready for receiving data and to perform error control in communication modes ⓐ to ⓓ .

Figure 8.1 Interface description of printer interface.

Pin No.	Signal	Direction	Description
12	–	---	Unused
13	Signal ground (SG)	–	Signal ground
14 to 17	–	–	Unused
20 or * 11	Data terminal ready (DTR)	From printer	Signal to indicate printer is ready to operate.
9,10, 18,19, 21 to 25	–	–	Unused

*Receptacle pin numbers for SSD and DTR are selectable with jumper plugs SP1 and SP2 (refer to table on page **150**).

Figure 8.1   (*Continued*)

Pin-1 protective ground.   The *pin-1 protective ground* is also known as frame ground, chassis ground, or earth ground. As we have previously discussed, pin 1 is used to ensure that dangerous voltages do not exist between the chassis of the two devices connected by the interface cable. It is also used to reduce noise that can induce transmission errors.

Pin-2 TD from the printer; Pin-3 RD to the printer.   A connection to TD of the printer is required only in communications protocols, where the printer must send an ASCII handshaking code as in the X-ON/X-OFF flow control.

Pin-4 RTS; Pin-5 CTS.   *Pin-4 RTS* and *Pin-5 CTS* indicate that the printer uses standard RTS/CTS handshaking to enable the transmitter in its UART.

Pin-6 DTR; Pin-8 DCD.   The printer must see both these signals at an asserted level to enable the receiver in its UART. This requirement can be modified in the printer setup.

Pin-7 SG.   As usual, signal ground is the reference for all data and handshaking signals on the interface.

Pin 11 SSD; Pin-20 DTR.   In previous chapters we discussed how printers are capable of hardware handshaking on pin 20 or pin 11. The EIA did not assign a name to pin 11. Okidata Corporation calls it SSD, which stands for *supervisory send data*. This pin represents the state of the printer's buffer. SSD is at a spacing level to signify a buffer not full (printer ready) and a marking level to signify a full buffer (printer busy). Through a pair of jumpers, the SSD function can be assigned to either pin 20 or pin 11. Also note that the active state of SSD can be inverted; this enables SSD to function as either a printer-ready or a printer-busy indicator.

If SSD is assigned to pin 11, then pin 20 functions as a standard DTR pin. It is asserted to indicate that the printer is powered up and on-line. Later in this section we examine the possible combinations of pin 11 and pin 20 handshaking.

Page 140 lists the seven communications protocols supported by the RS-232 printer interface; Pages 142 through 146 describe the protocols in detail. You should note that we are already extremely familiar with printer-ready/busy protocol (standard DTR/pin-11 hardware handshaking) and X-ON/X-OFF flow control. The other protocols listed on page 140 are used to support less commonly implemented communications techniques; nevertheless, it is an excellent investment of your time to read pages 142 through 146 carefully.

The figure on page 141 illustrates the DCE-to-DTE straight-through printer cable that is easily constructed from simple ribbon cable and insulation displacement connectors. Figure 8.2 is a reproduction of the figure on page 142, which illustrates a partial DTE-to-DTE printer cable.

Note that TD from the printer is required only if X-ON/X-OFF flow control is implemented. RTS is looped back to CTS so the transmitter of the UART is always enabled. DTR is looped back to DSR, which enables the receiver whenever the printer is powered up and on-line. Figure 8.2 assumes that the SSD function is assigned to pin 11, which should drive DSR and DCD of the data source.

The notes under the section on protocols (p. 142) provide important information. The block-end code can be assigned to a CR or LF character. This code indicates the last character in a block of data. Typically this character is a CR and delimits a block of a maximum 256 characters.

The printer indicates a framing error by printing ^ and a parity error by printing @. This is important information to know for troubleshooting purposes; these

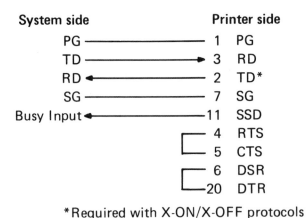

*Required with X-ON/X-OFF protocols

Figure 8.2   Okidata DTE to DTE partial cable.

characters are a de facto standard widely utilized throughout the printer and terminal industry.

The buffer size of the Okidata-92 is 2K, approximately one full screen of characters. Function switch 16 is used to implement the full buffer of 2K or a partial buffer of one block (256 bytes).

Figure 8.3 is a reproduction of page 148 and describes the first eight function switches on the interface board. These switches are used to set the type of parity, parity enable, number of data bits, baud rate, and block-end code. Note that if switch 2 is on, the setting of switch 1 is irrelevant. The advantage of selecting CR instead of LF as the block-end code is that an LF character can be suppressed to achieve overstrike and underline printing. Imagine sending a line of text appended with a CR character. The print head would return to the column of the current line. Underline or overstrike characters can be sent to the same line; the second printing of the line will be appended by both LF and CR.

Figure 8.4 is a reproduction of page 149 and describes functions switches 9 through 16. Switches 9 through 11 represent seven communications protocols and a

Function Switch	Description	Switch Settings	
		ON	OFF
1	Parity setting	Odd	Even
2	With/Without Parity	Without	With
3	Data Bit	7 bits	8 bits
4-7	Transmission Speeds	SW4 SW5 SW6 SW7 Baud ON OFF OFF OFF 9600 OFF ON ON ON 4800 OFF ON ON OFF 2400 OFF ON OFF ON 1200 OFF ON OFF OFF 600 OFF OFF ON ON 300 OFF OFF ON OFF 200 OFF OFF OFF ON 150 OFF OFF OFF OFF 110	
8	Block End Code	CR	LF

NOTE: CR or LF can be used as a block end code only in protocols (a), (b) or (g.)
To enable the serial interface, SW8 on the Operator Panel must be set to ON.

Figure 8.3 Communications specification setup.

Function Switch	Description	Switch Settings	
		ON	OFF
9–11	Protocol	SW9 SW10 SW11 Mode ON ON ON a OFF ON ON b ON OFF ON c OFF OFF ON d ON ON OFF e OFF ON OFF f ON OFF OFF g OFF OFF OFF test	
12	Changes DTR function	To use DTR to indicate when printer power is ON	To use DTR to indicate when printer is in SEL or DE-SELECT or if printer has paper
13,14	Changes polarity of SSD	BUSY is SPACE (High)	BUSY is MARK (Low)

NOTE: For systems using protocols (a), (b), (c), (d), and (e), switches 13 and 14 allow you to select SPACE or MARK signals to satisfy your system's requirements. To verify that your system is monitoring the printer's SSD signal, try running the printer with switches 13 and 14 ON, then the next time with them OFF. The printer should run correctly with one setting and not at all with the other. If the printer operates in both settings, the SSD pin is connected to the wrong system pin.

Function Switch	Description	ON	OFF
15	Changes function of CD signal	CD must be SPACE (High) to receive data	Printer ignores CD, Pin #8
16	Block length*	2K	256

*SW16 can be used to change the level of the maximum data length of one block including the transmission control code. For protocols (a), (b), (c), (e) and (f), setting SW16 in the ON position specifies a block length of 2048 characters or less, whereas setting SW16 in the OFF position specifies a block length of 256 characters or less.

For protocols (d) and (g), there is no block length limit.

Figure 8.4 Protocol, handshaking, and buffer select.

test setting. Usually mode a (SSD hardware handshaking) or mode g (X-ON/X-OFF flow control) is selected.

The setting of switch 12 assumes that pin 11 will be used as the SSD output. When switch 12 is on, a spacing level on DTR indicates only that the printer is powered up; when switch 12 is off, a spacing level on DTR indicates that the printer is powered up, on-line, and has paper. This is a much more comprehensive implementation of DTR.

Switches 13 and 14 set the active polarity of SSD. An active level on SSD can be defined as representing a printer-busy (both switches on) or printer-ready (both switches off). Because SSD is used to drive DSR and/or DCD of the data source, switches 13 and 14 are usually in the off position. When the printer buffer is full, SSD will go to an inactive marking level, forcing DSR and/or DCD of the data source inactive, which in turn sets the data source into a wait state. Carefully read the note to prove to yourself that you thoroughly understand the subtle difference between printer-ready and printer-busy handshaking.

Switch 15 defines whether DCD will actually be monitored by the printer. For direct-connect applications, this switch is set to the off position, causing the printer to ignore the state of DCD. Notice in Figure 8.2 that DCD is not illustrated in the direct-connect DTE-to-DTE cable.

Switch 16 permits the setting of a maximum block length of 2K or 256 bytes. Most computers will not send blocks in excess of 256 characters. As the note states, the setting of switch 16 is used to provide a maximum block length for most of the supported protocols.

Figure 8.5 is a reproduction of the jumper plug function table on page 150.

JUMPER PLUG FUNCTIONS

Jumper Plug #	Function	Side A	Side B
SP1, SP2	selection of receptacle pin number for SSD, DTR	SSD=11 pin DTR=20 pin	SSD=20 pin DTR=11 pin
SP3	selection of +5V current supply to receptacle pin #18	not supplied	supplied

IMPORTANT: SP1 and SP2 must be set to the same side. Otherwise, the printer could be damaged.

Figure 8.5 SSD function-select jumpers.

Two jumpers are used to select whether pin 20 or pin 11 is assigned the function of SSD or DTR. Normally SSD is assigned to pin 11 and DTR to pin 20. This provides the maximum printer-status information to the data source. The other jumper plug is used to connect a +5-V power supply to pin 18 of the RS-232 interface, a function that is rarely used.

8.3 TESTING THE PRINTER

Most printers have on-board self-tests in firmware (ROM). Typically, a self-test is invoked by depressing and holding the line-feed switch on the front panel of the printer and then turning on the AC power. The printer should respond by continuously printing its entire character set; this tests the print head, mechanical components, and microprocessor-controlled logic board. However, it should be fully understood that this test does not verify the operation of the RS-232 interface.

Page 154 illustrates the local loop-back test function as it is invoked on the Okidata-92. A BOB can easily be configured to emulate the test connector. Function switches 9 through 11 are turned to off positions to instigate the self-test mode. When the printer is powered on, the indications listed on page 154 should be printed. This verifies the operation of the UART, line drivers and receivers, and buffer memory and proper connection to the printer's logic board.

8.4 TESTING THE SYSTEM

You have now verified that the serial adapter in the PC and the serial interface in the printer are correctly installed and operational. Each connector on the interface cable should be securely connected. Be cautious! If the cable is not symmetrical, ensure that it is correctly installed.

Before the IBM-PC can send data to the printer, the communications parameters of the serial interface must be set. This operation can be accomplished in two different ways. An applications program such as a word-processing package or spreadsheet may have a setup program that asks the user to supply information about the type of printer (to install the proper driver), type of interface (parallel or serial), and (if a serial interface is indicated) the typical communications parameters.

The other procedure (which is more convenient for testing and troubleshooting purposes) uses the *PC-DOS mode* command. The PC-DOS operating system provides many utility programs that enable the user to interact quickly and efficiently with the microcomputer's hardware. In addition to the many other functions it provides, the PC-DOS mode command is used to set the communications parameters of the serial ports. The basic structure of the Mode command is:

```
Mode COMn: baud rate, parity, data bits, stop bits, P-option
```

COMn: is the name of the COMmunications port. The PC supports two communications ports, COM1: and COM2:.

The possible baud rates are:

110, 150, 300, 600, 1200, 2400, 4800, or 9600

Parity is indicated as N(none), O(odd), or E(even).

Data bits are selected as 7 or 8.

Stop bits can be selected as 1 or 2. One stop bit is selected for all except the lowest baud rates that indicate extremely slow electromechanical devices, which require a lengthy recovery time.

If the COM port is connected to a modem, the P-option is not used and the driver quickly times out and issues an error condition if DSR or CTS are not asserted. If the P-option is used, the communications port driver does not issue a time-out error but continues to poll the DSR and CTS status lines. This enables the printer to drive the DSR line with the equivalent to the Okidata SSD signal and not have a buffer-full condition interpreted as an error.

Assume that you have set the printer to 9600 baud, even parity, with CR block code as indicated in Figure 8.3. By executing the command

```
Mode COM1:9600,e,8,1,p
```

the computer and printer can now communicate. There are many ways to send data to the printer. The simplest method is to find or create an ASCII file with no control characters (except LF and CR) and redirect I/O to the printer. This is accomplished by using the PC-DOS command "Type filename." Type sends (types) the contents of a file on the video display. To send the contents of the selected file to the printer, simple I/O redirection is employed. Assume that we have an ASCII file called test.doc. The command

```
Type test.doc > COM1:
```

sends the contents of "test.doc" to COM1: (Note that the colon must follow COM1.) The ">" says "instead of sending the contents of the file to the video display, redirect it to COM1:." The file should be correctly printed. This tests only that the handshaking lines are all asserted, the communications setup is correct, and portions of the interface cable are operating correctly. This does not check the buffer-full printer handshaking; longer files must be used for that purpose.

8.5 TROUBLESHOOTING THE INTERFACE

What are the most likely problems that will cause the printer not to work properly or even not to function at all? The following list of routine checks should be performed in the event of a malfunctioning computer/printer interface:

1. Check the settings of the baud rate, number of data bits, stop bits, parity, handshaking, and protocol switches on the printer.

2. Execute the mode command to guarantee that the parameters set in Step 1 are exactly duplicated on the microcomputer.

3. Check the integrity of the interface cable connections on the computer and the printer: Are they snug and secured? Is the cable on backwards?

4. Execute the loop-back diagnostic test on the PC's serial port and the printer's internal self-test and loop-back test.

5. Insert a BOB into the interface cable with all switches closed. Check for marking levels on TD (pin 2) and RD (pin 3).

6. On the PC side of the interface, RTS and DTR should be asserted, with RTS driving CTS to a spacing level.

7. DSR and DCD on the PC side of the interface should be at an asserted level, driven by the printer-ready output.

8. On the printer side of the interface, RTS should drive CTS to an asserted level, and DTR should drive DSR to an asserted level.

9. Send an ASCII file to the COM port of the PC. The TD LED of the BOB should flicker slightly, indicating a stream of data bits.

10. Remove the interface cable and carefully inspect the plugs and sockets in the connectors for bent or broken pins.

11. Check for wires that are crimped on the insulation instead of conductor.

12. Check for broken wires.

13. Check the RS-232 connectors on the PC and printer for bent or broken pins.

With the aid of an ohmmeter, perform the following check:

14. Verify that the actual configuration of the wires in the cable corresponds to the planned design. Place one probe of the ohmmeter on TD of one connector and use the other probe to find its corresponding pin(s) on the other connector. This check not only maps out the physical cable but also detects opens (as the result of broken wires or miscrimped plugs) and shorts between wires that should not be connected.

8.6 TYPICAL SYMPTOMS AND SOLUTIONS

In this section we examine typical symptoms that indicate interface malfunctions and their causes and solutions.

Terminal connected to modem, or computer prints garbage or

@. This problem usually indicates that the terminal is set to the wrong baud rate. As you should remember, most terminal and printers use @ to indicate a parity error. When the baud rates between two devices are different, the receiver misinterprets the width of the bit cells and character frame. This results in what appears to be a parity error.

Other characters often printed due to the action of *slipping a frame* are x (111 1000), : (111 1100), and ˉ (111 1110). Notice that the ASCII codes of these characters have logic 1s in the most significant bits and logic 0s in the least significant bits.

Garbage is printed for a few characters and then everything is all right. This problem often occurs during the enabling and disabling of printer ports on RS-232 terminals. A control code or escape sequence is issued by the computer to enable the printer port. The microprocessor on the logic board of the terminal takes a finite length of time to enable the printer port. If this operation is too slow, then the first few characters are received out of frame and printed as random garbage. After a few characters the frame is resynced and characters are received and printed correctly.

The solution to this problem is surprisingly simple: Precede the text to be printed with one or two delete (111 1111) characters. In asynchronous communications, the ASCII DEL is used to recapture *frame synchronization*. To refresh your memory, Figure 8.6 depicts the RS-232 bit-stream representation of an ASCII DEL.

Notice that the ASCII DEL is nothing but a start bit! Most printers ignore delete characters; if the printer port is enabled before the bit stream is directed to the printer, then the leading deletes will be received and the printer operation will proceed as normal. Be assured that the addition of a parity bit to the ASCII DEL will not affect its ability to resync the frame.

If the printer port is enabled just as the bit stream is directed to the printer port, then the start bit will probably be sampled near the falling edge; the UART will resample the data line in the middle of the bit-cell and see an inactive marking level. The UART interprets this as a false start bit and waits for the start bit of the next character.

If the receiving UART is enabled after the DEL character is sent, the marking level of the seven logic 1 bits will appear as a conventional inactive line.

The printer misses the first few letters each time it is enabled. This problem is similar to the frame slip just discussed. The receiving UART may be enabled correctly, but the few characters are simply dropped and not printed. When this occurs, manufacturers recommend that the beginning of the print

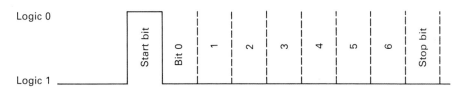

Figure 8.6   ASCII DEL (7FH).

message be padded with a few ASCII NUL characters. Like the DEL character, printers ignore the ASCII NUL.

The terminal or micro works for the first few lines when you log onto a mainframe but then starts printing garbage.

Consider the case where the port on the terminal or micro is inadvertently set for 2 stop bits when the computer with which it is conversing is set for 1 stop bit. To a receiver expecting 1 stop bit, a transmitter sending 2 stop bits does not cause any problems. The second stop bit merely looks like an inactive marking level.

The case where a receiver that is set (accidentally or because of circuit malfunction) to expect 2 stop bits but receives only 1 stop bit results in communication problems. The bit stream from a transmitter that is sending widely spaced characters with only 1 stop bit actually appears to be sending a large number of stop bits because of the long marking period of the inactive TD line between the character bursts. Figure 8.7 illustrates such a situation.

Notice that between the character frames there exists significant idle time on the TD line. This idle time appears to be extra stop bits. As long as the characters are widely spaced, as in Figure 8.7, even though the transmitter is only appending 1 stop bit to each character, there still appears to be at least 2 stop bits. Figure 8.8 depicts a situation where the transmitter buffers many characters and then sends them in a block. This is a more efficient use of computer time and is a widely practiced method of communicating with asynchronous terminals. Note that the 1 stop bit is now adjacent to the start bit of the next character; there is no idle line time to appear as extra stop bits.

Assume (for the sake of this problem description) that during the log-in process, a computer transmits data on a per-character basis; after the user is logged in, the computer then switches to a buffered I/O mode. If your terminal or microcomputer is accidentally set to 2 stop bits, the communication during the log-in process appears as normal because of the idle line time between characters. After you are logged in and the computer switches to buffered I/O, your receiver still expects to see 2 stop bits, but only 1 is being sent. Garbage appears on the video display because the receiver is operating on a frame than is 1 bit longer than the transmitter is sending.

Modem loses connection on an intermittent basis.

When you are connected to a remote computer via a modem, any interruption on the phone line may cause either the remote or local modem to drop the carrier. Consider the case

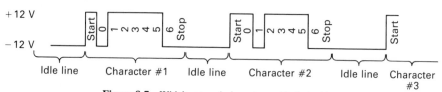

Figure 8.7 Widely spaced characters with 1 stopbit.

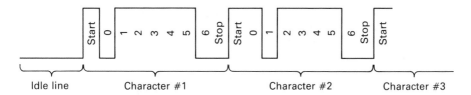

| Idle line | Character #1 | Character #2 | Character #3 |

Figure 8.8   Characters buffered and transmitted in a block.

where you have many phones in your house linked to a common phone line. If you are connected to a remote computer and someone picks up an extension phone, the disturbance on the phone line will cause your video display to fill quickly with garbage characters. If the phone is quickly replaced the connection will not be dropped, and the conversation with the remote computer will return to normal.

Telephone companies in most regions of the United States support a feature called *call waiting*. If you are busy with another conversation and an incoming call arrives, the call-waiting mechanism sounds a tone to indicate an incoming call. By clicking the cradle the present caller can be put on hold and the incoming call is switched onto the line. If you are using your modem at the time a call-waiting tone is sounded, it will drop the carrier and the connection will be lost. If you have intermittent problems with connections that are inexplicably dropped, check to see if you have call waiting.

Intermittent printer connection exists.   If your printer has intermittent problems, it may be related to the number of pins in the interface cable. When the connectors on the printer cable only have a few pins, they may not make reliable electrical contact with the pins on the equipment's connectors.

The solution to this problem is simply to add more pins or plugs to the connectors on the interface cable. These extra pins (without wires) add rigidity and mechanical support to the connection.

No earth ground exists.   Many terminals and computers are dependent on earth ground to set a reference for signal ground. Check terminals and microcomputers to ensure that they have not been connected to AC power with a three-prong to two-prong adapter whose ground tab is not connected to the screw on the outlet cover. Another common problem concerns the use of two-wire extension cords. Users often plug a computer or terminal into a two-wire extension cord via a three-prong to two-prong adapter. This robs the equipment of earth ground, which may not only affect the device's operation but also cause a dangerous situation for the operator.

Two problems that we have already discussed but that merit another reference are the half-duplex/full-duplex and CR/LF–CR only problems. If you are connected to a remote computer and everything that you type appears twice but every character the computer originates appears only once, you are set to half-duplex and the remote computer is set to full-duplex. If every line on your video display is double-spaced, then your computer is appending an LF to every CR it receives, as is the remote computer; change the setup to CR only. If only one line appears on the video display and it is constantly overwritten, then change the setup from CR only to CR/LF.

As we discussed in the previous chapter, the symptom of a printer that prints the first part of a long document correctly but starts printing garbage after a few pages indicates that the computer is not correctly handshaking with the printer. Check the setup of both devices and also check the interface cable to ensure that it has the correct pins to support printer ready or X-ON/X-OFF handshaking.

8.7 TROUBLESHOOTING THE ELECTRONICS
ON THE INTERFACE BOARD

This section considers some of the more common component failures that occur on serial interface boards. These checks require the use of a DMM and an oscilloscope.

Consider the situation where your terminal or microcomputer will not converse with a 1200-baud modem. The following are some of the checks that are normally executed:

1. Verify the interface circuitry on the RS-232 interface of the terminal with a loop-back plug.
2. Place a BOB into the interface cable and ensure that the correct handshaking signals are generated.
3. Verify the setup of the terminal and modem.

After these three steps are executed, the functionality of the modem may still be in question. The modem and interface cable should be tested on a different terminal to verify their operation. If the modem and cable work on another terminal, then you may seem to have an impossible situation. Notice that the loop-back test on the terminal verifies the correct operation of the UART and line drivers and receivers, but it does not guarantee that you are actually set at the correct baud rate.

Sometimes baud-rate setup switches malfunction or the documentation is incorrect. (The latter case is true more often than you would think.) How can we empirically derive the baud rate of a terminal or micro? Remember that the inverse of the baud rate is equal to the period of 1 bit cell. Refer to Figure 8.9, which indicates the period of a bit cell at 1200 baud.

Set the time base of the oscilloscope so 3 or 4 bit cells are displayed. The vertical deflection should be 5 V/Div and the triggering mode should be set to *NORM*. In the NORM trigger mode, the beam does not sweep until a trigger is sensed. This results in a much more stable display than employing the standard *AUTO trigger* mode. Depress and hold down a key whose ASCII code is an alternation of 1s and 0s. The author prefers U (101 0101) because the first data bit is a logic 1, the opposite of the logic 0 spacing-level start bit. The inverse of the period of a bit cell (as indicated on the oscilloscope) is the baud rate of the transmitter.

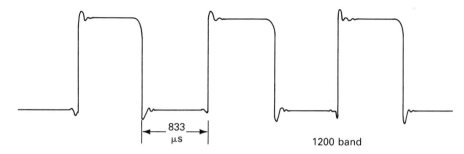

Figure 8.9   Empirically deriving baud rate.

Consider the following symptom: The terminal or micro connected to a mainframe computer by means of a long transmission cable works with a loop-back plug but functions intermittently when communicating with the computer.

Sometimes RS-232 line drivers get weak and become incapable of driving long, highly capacitive transmission lines. The easiest way to test for this type of failure is to measure the TD to SG short circuit current.

Set your DMM to read DC current on the 20 mA scale. Connect a BOB to the RS-232 port of the terminal or microcomputer. Connect one lead of the DMM to TD and the other lead to SG. This shorts the marking level on TD to SG via the DMM. An RS-232 line driver powered with ± 12 V typically has a mark-to-ground short-circuit current of 7 mA and a space-to-ground short-circuit current of 8 mA. Any driver that cannot source at least 5 mA of short-circuit current may need to be replaced. Try this measurement on a few RS-232 ports and ensure that your empirical readings are consistent with the author's.

As a corollary to the weak driver problem, consider the typical symptoms exhibited by devices that are connected by an RS-232 interface cable that is too long and has an excessive amount of capacitance. Connect the oscilloscope to TD on the remote end of the interface cable. Have another person (or use a piece of folded computer card to) hold down a selected key on the terminal. Observe the degraded TD signal. If the signal appears like the one in Figure 8.10 you have three possible solutions: slow down the baud rate, employ a line driver, or replace the old interface cable with ultra-low capacitance cable.

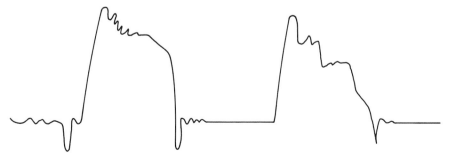

Figure 8.10   Excessively distorted RS-232 signal.

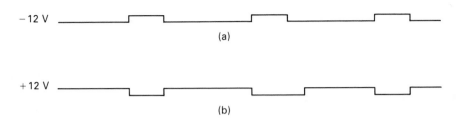

(a)

(b)

Figure 8.11 Malfunctioning −12-V or +12-V power supplies.

Always keep in mind that an open input will be interpreted by a line receiver as an inactive marking level. On the IBM-PC this is not always true because of the wide hysteresis line receivers employed.

Figure 8.11 illustrates the waveform of TD when the interface card has a power-supply malfunction. Note that the signals are stuck at the level of the correctly functioning power supply. Figure 8.11(a) and (b) indicates small glitches where the line driver attempts to change states.

Figure 8.12 illustrates an interesting situation. What happens when the outputs of two line drivers are shorted together? This situation results from an incorrectly designed or manufactured interface cable, bent pins, or solder bridges on the interface board.

In cases A and B in Figure 8.12, the drivers are both in agreement and output the same logic levels. In case C one driver is outputting a space and the other is outputting a mark. Neither driver actually wins—the resulting voltage is approximately 2 V to 3 V, resulting in an indeterminate level.

The waveform in Figure 8.12 is positive indication of shorted drivers. Disconnect the interface cable and check for bent pins on the connectors or the equipment and cable. If this does not reveal the problem, check the integrity of the interface cable with an ohmmeter. Finally, attach the BOB directly to each piece of equipment and check for continuity between outputs. This may indicate a short that is on an interface board.

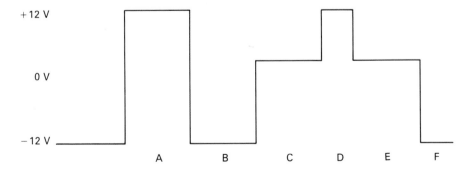

Figure 8.12 Shorted line drivers.

8.8 VERIFYING THE CONTINUITY OF A LONG INTERFACE CABLE

Imagine the situation where you have pulled a 500-ft interface cable through walls and ceilings to connect a terminal to a computer. This cable is illustrated in Figure 8.13. The cable has four wires, color coded red, green, yellow, and black. The terminal and computer will not converse. The computer port is checked out and functions properly; another terminal has been substituted and the same symptoms occur. These symptoms may induce characters such as ˜, x, and : occurring randomly on the video display. We know that these characters often indicate a baud-rate mismatch, but they can also indicate an open RD line.

Figure 8.13   Two-pair cable.

It is your job to verify the interface cable. Remembering that it is 500 ft long, how can you check out the continuity of each wire? One method is illustrated in Figure 8.14. A jumper cable with alligator clips or easy hooks is used to jumper two wires on the remote end of the cable. An ohmmeter is then employed to check for continuity. This verifies that both wires jumpered are continuous.

Assume that we have shorted the red and green wires and the ohmmeter indicates an open. How can we detect which of the two wires are open? We can jumper the red wire to the black wire and check for continuity and then repeat the process for the green wire. If all four wires are open due to the cable being completely severed, then all combinations of shorted pairs will read open.

Figure 8.15 indicates a method that checks for continuity on a wire-by-wire basis. This method assumes that earth ground is easily accessed at both ends of the interface cable. Earth ground can be found as the third plug in an AC outlet or by jumpering to a cold-water pipe. The first wire is shorted to ground at the remote end of the cable. The ohmmeter should now show continuity with earth ground. As the jumper on the remote end is removed, the ohmmeter should indicate an open circuit.

Figure 8.14   Jumpering two wires together.

Figure 8.15   Checking continuity by employing earth ground.

Consider the situation where you have a cable with four wires spanning a great distance through many different jumpering panels. You are not even sure that the color code of each wire in the cable is consistent. Furthermore, you need to perform the verification of the cable without the aid of a second person. Figure 8.16 illustrates a simple way to accomplish such a task. Figure 8.16(a) depicts a simple test connector constructed from four resistors of different values. Notice that the resistors on one side of the test connector are common (tied together.)

Figure 8.16(b) illustrates the manner in which the test connector is employed. Each wire on the remote end of the cable is connected to one of the resistors, and the common end of the test connector is jumpered to earth ground. On returning to the local end of the cable, the resistance to ground of each wire is measured. This

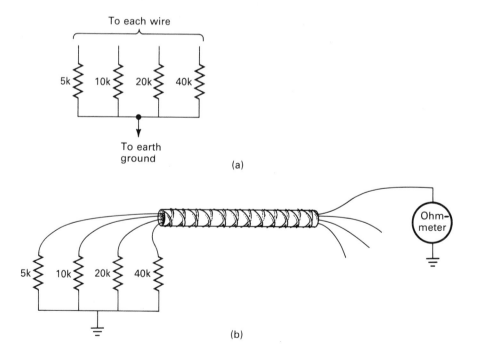

Figure 8.16   Resistor method of identifying wires.

uniquely identifies each wire and also verifies continuity. It does not matter what values of resistors are selected as long as they are significantly different.

These important concepts summarize the material in Chapter 8:

- Contrary to the industry standard, the IBM-PC asynchronous communications adapter has a male connector.
- The native BIOS on the IBM-PC does not support X-ON/X-OFF.
- The UART employed by the IBM-PC does not have hardware-dependent handshaking requirements. It is completely up to the driver program to manipulate the RTS and DTR outputs and interpret the state of the CTS, DSR, and DCD inputs.
- The compensation inputs of the 75154 line receiver used in the IBM-PC are tied to $+5$ V. A floating input does appear as a marking level; the last legitimate input level is latched on the outputs of the line receiver.
- The IBM Advanced Diagnostics Diskette contains a loop-back program to test the RS-232 interface.
- Many printers can be configured to handshake on DTR or pin 11.
- The block-end code is usually a CR.
- Printers print @ to indicate a parity error and ⌢ to indicate a framing error.
- The PC-DOS mode command can be used to set the communications parameters on the serial port.
- I/O redirection is used to guide the output away from the standard console (video display) to an alternative output device.
- Remember: Because a printer successfully outputs a short document does not necessarily mean that the handshaking is working properly.
- Section 8.5 describes 14 steps that should be performed in the event of a malfunctioning computer-printer interface.
- Section 8.6 lists many typical symptoms and their solutions.
- ASCII DEL is used to recapture frame synchronization.
- ASCII NUL is used to pad print messages when the leading characters are dropped.
- Call waiting can cause the modem to drop the carrier.
- Two-wire extension cords may cause functional problems as well as allowing potentially dangerous voltages to exist on the chassis of an electronic device.
- To derive the baud rate of a data source empirically, measure the period of 1 bit cell. The inverse of that measurement is the baud rate.
- An RS-232 driver shorted to signal ground will source approximately 7 mA on a mark and 8 mA on a space.
- An oscilloscope can be used to observe the degradation of signals on a long RS-232 interface cable.

- An RS-232 TD line that is struck at $+12$ V or -12 V with small glitches may indicate a power-supply failure.
- Shorted drivers pulling in opposite directions result in an indeterminate voltage level.
- Three popular methods of verifying the integrity of cables are the jumper method, the ground method, and the resistor method.

High Speed Serial
Printer Interface

INTRODUCTION

This appendix describes the optional RS232-C high speed serial interface board which is available with OKIDATA Microline 92. The High Speed RS232-C gives the Microline 92 the capability of interfacing with virtually every personal computer system on the market today and enables the printer to receive data transmitted at speeds up to 9600 baud.

NOTE: With data transmission speeds of 4800 or more, the printer will not receive and print data simultaneously. There will be short delays in printing while the printer's buffer fills with data.

The High Speed RS232-C serial interface, which is mounted on a printed circuit board, is a factory-installed option in our Microline 92 printers. If you have a Microline 92 with a parallel interface and wish to change it to the RS232-C, the serial interface board can be purchased and easily installed. See Page A-18 for installation instructions.

The RS232-C interface provides communication in your choice of seven different protocols, including the popular X-ON/X-OFF and Printer Ready/Busy modes.

We suggest you read the following instructions before attempting to interface your printer with your computer. We also recommend that you review your system manual for sections on data transmission, protocols and wiring before connecting the printer to your system. Should you have any problems operating your printer after reading these instructions, please consult your dealer.

BEFORE YOU BEGIN

1) Familiarize yourself with both your printer and system user's manuals before attempting to install or operate your High Speed RS232C interface.

2) Make sure your printer and your system's power switches are in the OFF position before connecting interface cables or changing function switches.

3) Make sure all interface cables are properly wired. Damage may occur to your system if pins are improperly connected.

4) The interface connection cable must be securely connected to both the system and the printer before operating.

PRINTER INTERFACING REQUIREMENTS

Connectors

- Cable Side:

   25-pin plug
   Equivalent to DB-25P (Cannon)

- Shell:

   Equivalent to DB-C2-J9 (Cannon)

Cabling

   Maximum length 50 feet (15 meters)
   Shielded cable made of four twisted-pair wire conductors

NOTE: After connecting the cable assembly to the system and printer, fasten the connectors securely with the lock screws.

INTERFACING

Most interfacing cables are available from your dealer. If you are making your own cable, refer to this appendix for technical information regarding the High Speed RS232-C interface.

If your dealer cannot provide the information you need, contact us:

OKIDATA CORPORATION
Technical Support Group
111 Gaither Drive
Mount Laurel, New Jersey 08054

or call

(609) 235-2600 and ask for
TECHNICAL SUPPORT

INTERFACING CONNECTION METHOD

If you are making your own serial interface cable, familiarize yourself with the minimum signals required, then follow the step-by-step procedure to match your system with your OKIDATA printer. Below is a list of the most commonly used signals which will assist you in determining the correct pin connections. A table outlining all interface signals follows this section.

Signal	EIA	Description
PG	AA	This signal is pin #1 and is connected to eliminate noise in transmission as well as to prevent electrical shock in case of a short circuit. Your system documentation may also describe this as: FG Frame Ground CG Chassis Ground EG Earth Ground or PG Protective Ground
TD	BA	This signal is serial data being transmitted from one device to another. The TD (Transmit Data) line on your system will probably be pin #2 or #3, and may also be labeled XMIT data or TXD. This line must always be connected to the printer's pin #3, receive data line.
RD	BB	This signal is serial data received by a device and may also be labeled REC data or RXD. Your system's receive data line does not have to be connected to the printer's TD line, pin #2, unless you are running in the X-ON/X-OFF or STX/ETX protocols.
DTR	CD	This is probably pin #20 on your system. The Data Terminal Ready line is used to monitor the printer's busy line. In most applications, your system's DTR line will be connected to the printer's pin #11, busy line. If your system does not have a DTR line, connect the printer's pin #11 to your system's CTS pin.
CTS	CB	This pin is also commonly used to monitor your printer's busy line, pin #11, when your system does not have a DTR line.

Signal	EIA	Description
DSR	CC	This pin is used by the system to notify the printer that the system is ready for transmission and is connected to the printer's pin #11 when your system does not have a DTR or a CTS signal.
SSD*	—	This signal is the printer's pin #11 and, as indicated earlier, is also referred to as printer busy. This line becomes active when the printer's buffer is full and can no longer receive data from your computer. This pin will usually be connected to your system's pin #20. Refer to the function switch settings for more information regarding this line.

*OKIDATA printers provide this SSD signal on pin #11 to prevent buffer over-run situations where several characters or lines of data can be lost. If your system does not use this signal, all data sent to the printer when it is busy will be lost. EIA has not assigned a standard abbreviation for this signal.

Some systems use RTS as a busy signal.

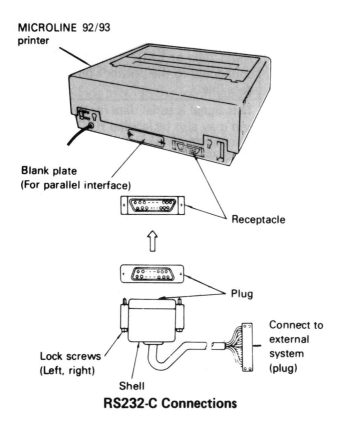

RS232-C Connections

RS232C SERIAL INTERFACE SIGNALS

Pin No.	Signal	Direction	Description
1	Protective ground (PG)	–	Connected to printer frame (frame ground)
2	Transmitted data (TD)	From printer	Serial data signal transmitted from printer
3	Received data (RD)	To printer	Serial data signal received by printer
4	Request to send (RTS)	From printer	Transmission request signal from printer. SPACE during trans-mission.
5	Clear to send (CTS)	To printer	Reply signal to RTS signal. Printer trans-mits data after con-firming this signal as SPACE.
6	Data set ready (DSR)	To printer	Signal to notify printer that trans-mitter is ready for transmission. Printer receives data after confirming this signal as SPACE.
7	Signal ground (SG)	–	Signal ground
8	Carrier detect (CD)	To printer	For MODEM connec-tion only: this signal is connected to the modem CD signal. Printer receives data after confirming this signal as SPACE.
11 or * 20	Supervisory send data (SSD)	From printer	Signal to indicate that the printer is not ready for receiving data and to perform error con-trol in communication modes (a) to (d) .

Pin No.	Signal	Direction	Description
12	–	---	Unused
13	Signal ground (SG)	–	Signal ground
14 to 17	–	–	Unused
20 or * 11	Data terminal ready (DTR)	From printer	Signal to indicate printer is ready to operate.
9,10, 18,19, 21 to 25	–	–	Unused

*Receptacle pin numbers for SSD and DTR are selectable with jumper plugs SP1 and SP2 (refer to table on page A-17).

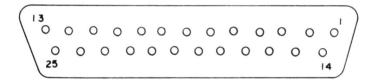

Receptacle Pin Arrangement

STANDARD PIN CONNECTIONS

NOTE: Refer to your system documentation before attempting to connect the pins according to the instructions below, since some popular computer systems do not conform to the RS232 standard. Okidata provides cabling information for most popular computer systems in a publication entitled "USER'S TIPS" which should be available from your dealer.

1) Cable Assembly:

To assemble the cable you will need two 25-pin male connectors (equivalent to a Cannon DB-25P), plus the connector shells, which act as a cable strain relief to help prevent wire breakage, and at least a four-conductor cable. This cable should not exceed 50 feet (15 meters) in length and a shielded cable with twisted pair conductors is desirable. Connect the pins according to your system and printer interface requirements. Stranded wire conductors are less subject to breakage when the cable is moved than the solid wire connectors.

2) DCE vs. DTE:

If your system documentation does not identify your computer as either a DCE (Data Communication Equipment) or a DTE (Data Terminal Equipment), it probably is set up as a DCE, acting as a controller.

The Microline 92 is set up as a DTE, the peripheral. Try arranging the pins according to the following instructions for a DCE to DTE interface. If your system does not operate after connecting the cable to the printer, rewire the cable following the DTE to DTE instructions.

3) Selecting protocol:

After you have studied your system manual to determine what protocol it operates under, you can select one of the following protocols:

NOTE: These protocols are explained in more detail on page A-9.

(a) Printer Ready/Busy
    (Oki Simplex Busy)

(b) Printer Ready/Busy-ACK
    (Oki Simplex Acknowledge)

(c) SOH/ETX
    (Centronics RS-232)

(d) Printer Ready Busy
    (Centronics Unblocked)

(e) STX/ETX
    (Centronics Blocked Simplex)

(f) STX/ETX-ACK
    (Centronics Blocked Duplex)

(g) X-ON/X-OFF
    (DEC Duplex)

4) Using flat connection cables:

If your system operates as a DCE to DTE, you can obtain a flat 25-pin connection cable and connect pin-for-pin without changing the wiring.

5) DCE to DTE connections:

Connections for protocols (a) , (b) , (c) , (d) and (e), are wired as follows to meet the printer's requirements.

System side   Printer side

PG ─────────────── 1 PG (Protective Ground)

*TD ◄────────────── 2 TD (Transmit Data)

RD ──────────────► 3 RD (Receive Data)

RTS ◄────────────── 4 RTS (Request to Send)

CTS ──────────────► 5 CTS (Clear to Send)

DSR ──────────────► 6 DSR (Data Set Ready)

SG ─────────────── 7 SG (Signal Ground)

DTR ◄─────────────20 DTR (Data Terminal Ready)

*Required for X-ON/X-OFF protocol

NOTE: Although pin #3 is always labeled the Receive Data line, this line actually permits the DCE to TRANSMIT to the DTE.

You will note that all pin connections are straight across — although you have a choice between connecting pins #4 or pins #20, depending on which line the computer monitors the printer's busy signal.

If your system does not monitor the printer's busy line on pin #4 or #20, connect the printer's pin #11, SSD line, to the system's designated monitoring line. The polarity of the SSD line is regulated by the setting of switches 13 and 14 on the high-speed board.

NOTE: Receptacle pin numbers on the printer side for the SSD (Busy) and DTR signals can be selected as either pin #11 or pin #20 by switching jumper plugs SP1 and SP2 (refer to the jumper plug function table on page A-17).

Consult your system documentation to determine cabling requirements which may require jumpers on the system side.

NOTE: Only systems using protocols (f) or (g) require the connection on pin #2, Transmit Data. However, since some systems require protocol changes with updated software packages, connecting this line now can make recabling for future applications unnecessary.

6) DTE to DTE Connections:

A small percentage of minicomputers are set up as a DTE. Since the printer is also wired as a DTE, the configuration will look like the following.

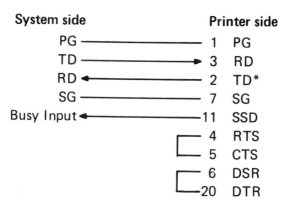

System side   Printer side

PG ————————————— 1 PG
TD —————————————→ 3 RD
RD ←————————————— 2 TD*
SG ————————————— 7 SG
Busy Input ←——————————11 SSD
                        ⌐ 4 RTS
                        ∟ 5 CTS
                        ⌐ 6 DSR
                        ∟20 DTR

*Required with X-ON/X-OFF protocols

In this case, as with most DTE to DTE configurations, the Transmit Data signal, pin #2, is connected to the printer's Receive Data signal, pin #3.

Consult your system manual for wiring requirements and jumper connections on the system side.

PROTOCOLS

A choice of seven protocols is available with the High-Speed RS232 Serial Interface Board for the Microline 92. Check your system documentation to determine the type of protocol your system operates under, then match it with the protocols we have listed below. Once you have identified the protocol you need, set the function switches on the RS232 board accordingly. Please note that the following symbols and their corresponding meanings are used interchangeably throughout this section.

1. LF or CR = Block End Code
2. ^   = Framing Error
3. @   = Parity Error
4. 2K = Buffer Size

NOTE: When data transmission speed is set for 4800 baud or higher, the printer cannot receive and print data simultaneously.

NOTE: Refer to the table concerning function switches on pages A-15 to A-16. The block end code (CR or LF) is selected with SW8. The maximum length of a block of data is selected with SW16: the ON position selects 2047 bytes, the OFF position selects 256 bytes.

ⓐ Printer Ready/Busy (OKI Simplex BUSY)

If SW16 is ON, the printer will receive data until a CR or LF is received. Then the printer will send the busy signal until the buffer is emptied. If SW16 is OFF, the printer permits the computer to transmit data until the printer buffer can hold only one more block of data containing 256 characters.

The printer then searches for a carriage return (CR) or line-feed (LF) command and, upon receipt, sends out a busy signal within 5 ms to advise the computer to stop transmitting until the buffer is empty. When a parity or framing error occurs, it is substituted by the @ or ^ sign respectively. The SSD signal is held ON when the printer is deselected.

For baud rates of 4800 or higher, the busy signal turns ON within 5 ms after receiving the block end code, and remains on until whatever was in the buffer is printed.

RS232 interface board function switch settings for Printer Ready/Busy:

SW9	ON
SW10	ON
SW11	ON

(b) Printer Ready/Busy-ACK (OKI Simplex ACK)

Permits the computer to transmit data until the printer's buffer can hold no more data. Each block of data transmitted cannot exceed either 2048 or 256 bytes according to the setting of SW16.

Each time a block of data and the block end code are transmitted to the printer, the printer responds with a busy signal for 200 ms to acknowledge that the transmission was received. When there are fewer than 256 character spaces left in the buffer, the printer's busy signal will remain ON until the buffer is emptied. If SW16 is ON, the busy signal stays on until the buffer is empty regardless of the amount of characters in the buffer.

While the printer is deselected, the busy signal turns ON when a block of data is received, and remains on until the printer is selected. The entire block of data is ignored if a framing or parity error is received; and the computer must retransmit the data if a busy signal is not received within a specified amount of time.

For data transmission speeds of 4800 baud or higher, the busy signal is turned ON within 5 ms after receiving a CR or a LF of a normal block, and remains ON until the buffer is empty and printing ends.

RS232 interface board function switch settings for Printer
Ready/Busy-ACK:

SW9	OFF
SW10	ON
SW11	ON

(c) SOH/ETX (Centronics RS232)

Each block of data begins with a Start of Header (SOH)
character and ends with an End of Text (ETX) character.
When the printer reads the ETX character, it sends a busy
signal to the computer for 200 ms. Each block of data must
be less than either 2048 or 256 bytes. If there are fewer
than 256 character spaces available in the buffer, the SSD
signal remains on for 200 ms after the receipt of the ETX
character. With SW16 ON: when an ETX code is received
the buffer is emptied before any more data can be received.

The busy signal is also on when the printer is deselected.
Parity and framing errors are substituted character-for-
character with the @ or ^ symbols. If an error occurs, the
SSD signal will not be turned on; the incorrect data with
errors is printed and the computer will have to retransmit the
data.

For data transmission speeds of 4800 baud or higher, the
busy signal turns ON within 5 ms after receiving the ETX,
and remains ON until the buffer becomes empty and printing
ends.

RS232 interface board function switch settings for SOH/
ETX:

SW9	ON
SW10	OFF
SW11	ON

(d) Printer Ready/Busy (Centronics Unblocked)

Permits data to be transmitted until there is only room left in
the buffer for 256 more characters. After the 256th character is received, a busy signal is sent by the printer to the
computer until the buffer is emptied. Parity and framing
errors are substituted by the @ or ^ signs.

The busy signal turns ON when the printer is deselected.

For data transmission rates of 4800 baud or higher, if no data is received within 200 ms when there is data in the buffer or when the buffer is full, the busy signal is turned ON within 5 ms and remains on until the buffer becomes empty and printing ends.

RS232 interface board function switch settings for Centronics Unblocked:

SW9	OFF
SW10	OFF
SW11	ON

⊛ STX/ETX (Centronics Blocked Simplex)

Each block of data begins with a Start of Text (STX) character and ends with an End of Text (ETX) character. All data outside of this block is ignored. When the printer reads the ETX character, it sends a busy signal to the computer for 200 ms. If an error occurs, the busy signal turns ON within 5 ms and remains on for 200 ms. All data in an error block is ignored, and the computer must retransmit the block of data.

NOTE: There is no busy signal for baud rates lower than 2400 baud.

For baud rates of 4800 and higher, the busy signal is turned ON 200 ms after ETX is received and remains ON until the buffer is empty and printing ends. If the printer is deselected, data is received until the buffer becomes full, and any additional data (overflow) is ignored.

RS232 interface board function switch settings for STX/ETX:

SW9	ON
SW10	ON
SW11	OFF

ⓕ STX/ETX-ACK (Centronics Blocked Duplex)

Blocks of data transmitted are limited to either 2047 or 256 bytes depending on the setting of SW16 and are identified by a Start of Text (STX) character in the beginning and an End of Text (ETX) character at the end of the block. When the ETX is received, a Request to Send (RTS) signal is sent by the printer to the computer. The computer sends a Clear to Send (CTS) signal and the printer, in response, transmits an acknowledge (ACK). If SW16 is OFF, the RTS signal is dropped when the next STX character is received.

If SW16 is ON, the RTS signal is dropped and transmission begins again only after the printer has printed the entire buffer.

When a parity error, framing error, or buffer overflow occurs, the printer will send a NAK code to notify the computer to retransmit the block of data.

There is no busy signal for baud rates of 2400 or lower.

For baud rates of 4800 and higher, when ETX of a normal block is received, RTS is turned ON and ACK sent. If the buffer is full, RTS remains ON until printing ends and the buffer is emptied. When the printer is deselected, data is received until the buffer is full, and overflow is lost until the printer is selected.

RS232 interface board function switch settings for STX/ ETX-ACK:

SW9	OFF
SW10	ON
SW11	OFF

⑨ X-ON/X-OFF (DEC Duplex)

Each block of data is identified by a CR or LF command (depending on the setting of switch 8) at the end of the block. There is no block length limitation. The printer becomes busy when there are fewer than 256 character spaces remaining in the buffer and sends an X-OFF (DC3) code to the computer.

When the buffer is cleared, the printer sends a X-ON (DC1) code. Framing and parity errors are substituted character-for-character with the @ or ^ symbols.

At data transmission speeds of 4800 baud or higher, the existence of data is monitored for 200 ms. If the buffer can hold 256 or fewer bytes, DC3 is sent. When the buffer is emptied and printing ends, DC1 is sent.

When the printer is deselected, DC3 is sent until the printer is selected again.

RS232 interface board function switch settings for X-ON/ X-OFF.

SW9	ON
SW10	OFF
SW11	OFF

RS232-C FUNCTION SWITCHES

The function switches on the RS232 High Speed serial interface board are set as follows before shipment from the factory. The table on the following pages gives details on all switch settings.

Switch	Position	Description
1	OFF	Even parity
2	ON	Without parity
3	OFF	8 bits
4	ON	
5	OFF	9600 baud
6	OFF	
7	OFF	
8	OFF	Block End Code = LF
9	OFF	
10	OFF	Printer Ready/Busy
11	ON	
12	OFF	DTR Signal
13	OFF	SSD-Mark (low) at Busy
14	OFF	
15	OFF	Ignores CD (Pin #5)
16	ON	2K Buffer

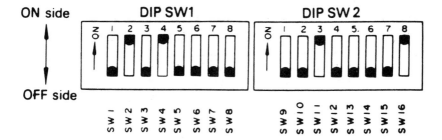

Factory Setting of Function Switches

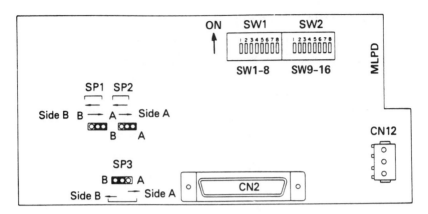

Layout of Switch Banks and Jumper Plugs

The following table lists the available functions and corresponding settings of the switches on the serial interface board.

Function Switch	Description	Switch Settings	
		ON	**OFF**
1	Parity setting	Odd	Even
2	With/Without Parity	Without	With
3	Data Bit	7 bits	8 bits
4–7	Transmission Speeds	SW4 SW5 SW6 SW7 Baud ON OFF OFF OFF 9600 OFF ON ON ON 4800 OFF ON ON OFF 2400 OFF ON OFF ON 1200 OFF ON OFF OFF 600 OFF OFF ON ON 300 OFF OFF ON OFF 200 OFF OFF OFF ON 150 OFF OFF OFF OFF 110	
8	Block End Code	CR	LF

NOTE: CR or LF can be used as a block end code only in protocols ⓐ, ⓑ or ⓖ. To enable the serial interface, SW8 on the Operator Panel must be set to ON (see page 22).

Function Switch	Description	Switch Settings ON	OFF
9–11	Protocol	SW9 SW10 SW11 Mode ON ON ON a OFF ON ON b ON OFF ON c OFF OFF ON d ON ON OFF e OFF ON OFF f ON OFF OFF g OFF OFF OFF test	
12	Changes DTR function	To use DTR to indicate when printer power is ON	To use DTR to indicate when printer is in SEL or DE-SELECT or if printer has paper
13,14	Changes polarity of SSD	BUSY is SPACE (High)	BUSY is MARK (Low)
NOTE: For systems using protocols ⓐ, ⓑ, ⓒ, ⓓ, and ⓔ, switches 13 and 14 allow you to select SPACE or MARK signals to satisfy your system's requirements. To verify that your system is monitoring the printer's SSD signal, try running the printer with switches 13 and 14 ON, then the next time with them OFF. The printer should run correctly with one setting and not at all with the other. If the printer operates in both settings, the SSD pin is connected to the wrong system pin.			
15	Changes function of CD signal	CD must be SPACE (High) to receive data	Printer ignores CD, Pin #8
16	Block length*	2K	256

*SW16 can be used to change the level of the maximum data length of one block including the transmission control code. For protocols ⓐ, ⓑ, ⓒ, ⓔ and ⓕ, setting SW16 in the ON position specifies a block length of 2048 characters or less, whereas setting SW16 in the OFF position specifies a block length of 256 characters or less.

For protocols ⓓ and ⓖ, there is no block length limit.

NOTE: If you are using a blocked protocol, return to text mode before terminating a block of dot-addressable graphics or of down-line loadable characters. Once in text mode, a block can be terminated with any terminator code such as CR, LF, ETX or EOT.

The control codes for character spacing and line spacing, CHR$(27);"N" and CHR$(27);"%9" respectively, cannot be followed by a terminator code.

JUMPER PLUG FUNCTIONS

Jumper Plug #	Function	Side A	Side B
SP1, SP2	selection of receptacle pin number for SSD, DTR	SSD=11 pin DTR=20 pin	SSD=20 pin DTR=11 pin
SP3	selection of +5V current supply to receptacle pin #18	not supplied	supplied

IMPORTANT: SP1 and SP2 must be set to the same side. Otherwise, the printer could be damaged.

INSTALLATION OF RS232-C BOARD

1. Turn your printer's A.C. power switch OFF and unplug the printer.

IMPORTANT: The printer's power switch must be OFF whenever the printer is plugged back in; otherwise, a power surge may cause damage.

2. Remove tractor unit or roll paper stand, if attached.

3. Remove the upper cover:
   - Remove the platen knob.
   - Remove the access cover by lifting it upward.
   - Using a Phillips screwdriver with at least a four-inch shaft, loosen the hold-down screws located inside the front of the upper cover.
   - Lift up the front of the upper cover and push it backward to release it from the hooks at the back of the base.

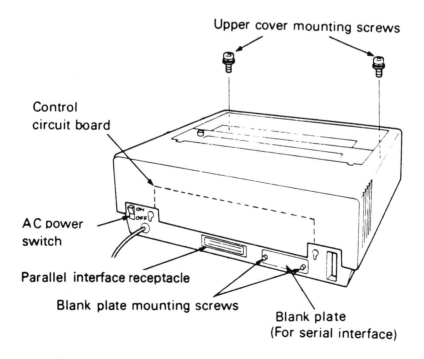

4. Loosen the screws on the parallel interface connector, then remove the locking hardware and retighten the screws.

5. Unfasten the two screws for the control circuit board and pull the board upward from slot A.

Refer to the figure below for steps 6 and 7.

6. Insert the 36-pin plug on the interface board into the 36-pin receptacle (CN 10) on the control circuit board.

7. Insert the two mounting posts mounted at the bottom of the interface board through the holes at the bottom of the control circuit board, and fasten them with the interface board mounting screws supplied with the board.

CAUTION: These screws act as a signal ground. If they are not connected the printer could be damaged.

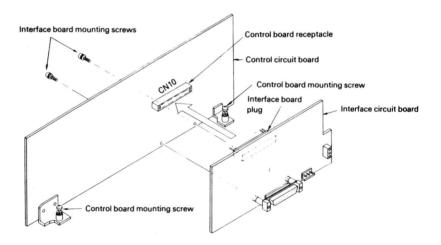

Refer to the figure below for steps 8 and 9.

8. Insert the control circuit board into slot A, the interface board into slot B, and tighten the two control board mounting screws.

9. Using the cable supplied with.your interface board, connect the 3-pin connector of the circuit board (CN11) with the 3-pin connector (CN11) on the interface board.

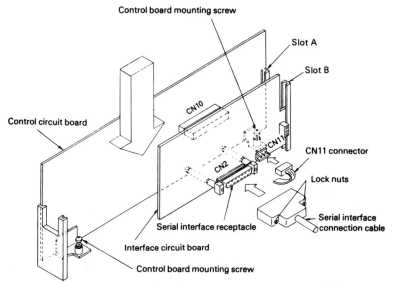

10. Set the function switches on the interface board according to your system's requirements. For an explanation of the function switches, see the table on page A-15 and A-16.

11. Set function switch #8 on the operator panel to ON. This activates the serial interface.

12. Remove the blank plate over the serial interface receptacle slot on the printer's rear panel, and place it over the parallel receptacle slot.

13. Replace the upper cover, access cover, and platen knob.

14. Connect the serial interface cable with the 25-pin receptacle (CN2). (Refer to figure on previous page.)

15. Make sure the printer has paper and ribbon.

16. Plug the printer in, then turn it ON, and check that the POWER and SEL lamps on the operator panel are lit. Now your printer is ready to receive data.

LOCAL TEST FUNCTION

If you want to make a test cable for the RS232-C interface board, follow the directions given on page A-6 for "Cable Assembly" and wiring connections provided below for your test cable.

Set the RS232-C interface board function switches as follows:

SW9	OFF
SW10	OFF
SW11	OFF

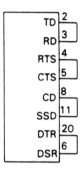

RS232 Test Connector Wiring Diagram

Connect the test connector to the interface connector.

To initiate the loop test, turn the printer's power ON. The serial will check the memory function of the printer's message buffer, the RS232-C interface driver, and the receiver circuit, then it will print all the characters.

Stop the test by turning the printer OFF.

The test printout includes the following:

1. "LOOP TEST" is printed.
2. "IF OK" is printed if the memory check is good.
   "IF BAD" is printed if the memory check is faulty.
3. Complete set of characters is printed.

If printer prints "IF BAD", there could be a problem between RTS and CTS.

If printing stops suddenly, then there could be a problem between TD and RD; DTR and DSR; or CD and SSD.

After running this test, reset the function switches for your protocol; disconnect the test cable and connect the interface cable.

RS232-C INTERFACE SPECIFICATIONS

Item	Description
Interface System	RS232-C
Data Input	Serial input Start-stop synchronization
Bit Rate	Up to 9600 baud
Data Word Length	7 or 8 bits
Parity	Odd, even or none
Number of Stop Bits	1 or more
Message Buffer Length	2K or 256
Communication Modes	Seven different protocols: a Printer Ready/Busy b Printer Ready/Busy--ACK c SOH/ETX d Printer Ready/Busy e STX/ETX f STX/ETX—ACK g X-ON/X-OFF one test mode
Interface Connector	Printer: 25-hole receptacle — Equivalent to Cannon DB-25S Cable: 25-pin plug — Equivalent to Cannon DB-25P Shell: Equivalent to Cannon DB-C2-J9

Power Supply
  (supplied by printer
   through cables)
	+35 V A.C., 20 mA
	+35 V D.C., 20 mA
	+5 V, 200 mA

RS232-C Signal Levels	+25 to +3 V D.C. SPACE (High) –25 to –3 V D.C. MARK (Low)

B Asynchronous RS-232 Terminal Operators Manual

The following appendix contains selected excerpts from the Televideo 925 Operators Manual. This information describes specific setup and operations procedures for an RS-232 terminal as discussed in Chapter 5.

1.1 INSTALLATION

1.1.1 Composite Video Jumper Option

To drive a monitor in addition to the terminal monitor, you can modify the 925 logic board. The logic board's part number may be labeled -001 or -002. The modification instructions for the composite video jumper are the same, regardless of the logic board designation.

The modifications needed are as follows:

1. Add a BNC connector to the back panel.
2. Connect the center lead to P2 pin 6; connect the ground lead of the BNC connector to P2 pin 3.
3. Cut the trace between E3 and E4 and install a jumper between E1 and E2.

1.1.2 Two-Page Memory Option

You can add one additional page of display memory to the 925. This is not normally factory-installed. Follow these steps to install this option:

1. Unplug the terminal and remove the top cover.
2. Install a 6116 2KX8 bit 150 NS RAM chip onto the control board. If the logic board is labeled -001, install the chip in position A48. If the board is labeled -002, install it in position A33.
   The notch on the chip should face the same direction as the notches on the other chips. Be careful not to bend the pins.
3. Check the notch position again before installing the cover and turning on power again.

TABLE 1–1   SERIAL
PRINTER INTERFACE
(P4) PIN
CONNECTIONS

Pin No.	Signal Name
1	Protect Ground
2	Receive Data
3	Transmit Data
4	Request To Send
5	Clear To Send
6	Data Set Ready
7	Signal Ground
8	Data Carrier Detect
20	Data Terminal Ready

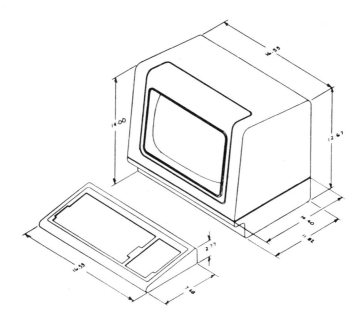

Figure 1–1   Model 925 Dimensions

1.1.3 Additional Field Modifications

The following field modifications may also be made. The directions given in this section apply to boards labeled -001 or -002.

1. For handshaking, use pin 4 (on P4) rather than pin 11 on P4. Cut the trace between E6 and E7 and install a jumper from E5 to E7.

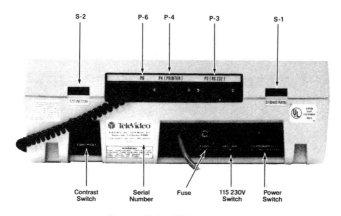

Figure 1–2   925 Rear Panel

2. To disconnect DTR from the printer (pin 20 on P4), cut the trace between E10 and E11.

3. To control DTR output (pin 20 on P3) with RTS output (pin 4 on P3), cut the trace between E15 and E16 and install a jumper between E14 and E16.

1.2 CHECKING YOUR INSTALLATION

Before you proceed to the next chapter and turn on the terminal, check to be sure you installed the terminal correctly.

1. Did you install the correct power plug for your wall outlet?
2. Did you set the power selector switch to match your power requirements?
3. Is the main interface cable to the computer system properly wired and plugged in?
4. If you are using a printer, did you plug in the printer interface connector?
5. Did you set the switches for the correct

   • baud rate (both for terminal and printer)?
   • stop bits?
   • word structure?
   • parity?

6. Did you set switches for

   • 50 or 60 Hertz (to match your powerline/frequency requirement)?
   • full or half duplex?

7. Did you plug the terminal in to the wall outlet?

If the answers are YES, then you are ready to proceed with actually using the terminal.

2.1 KEYBOARD CONTROL

2.1.1 Keyboard Layout

Figure 2–1 illustrates the keyboard layout. Refer to Table 2–1, where each key's function is described in detail. This table is subdivided by types of functions and gives information on the effect of each key and commands. For detailed information, refer to Table 2–1.

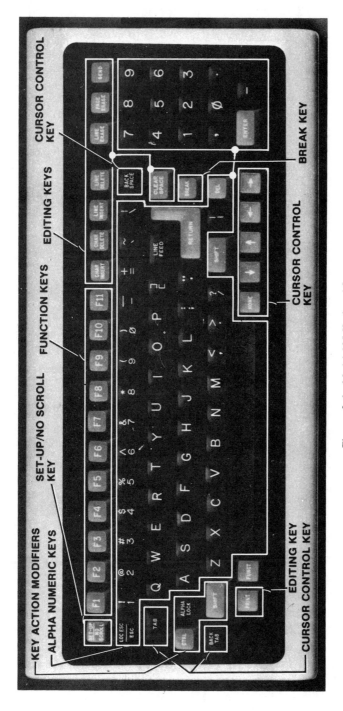

Figure 2-1 Model 925 Keyboard Layout

161

TABLE 2-1 FUNCTION OF KEYS

Key Name	Transmitted? (Yes/No)	Repeat Action? (Yes/No)	Description
Space Bar	Y	Y	Causes a blank space to appear on the display and transmits an ASCII space code (20 Hex).
SHIFT	N	N	Selects upper character inscribed on a key, changes operation of most special keys, and capitalizes alpha characters.
ALPHA LOCK	N	N	Locks the SHIFT keys so that all alpha keys transmit codes for upper-case characters. The key is pressed to lock and pressed again to release.
TAB	Y	Y	(CTRL/1—TAB moves the cursor forward to typewriter tabs (Protect mode off) or to the start of the next unprotected field (Protect mode on).
BACK TAB	Y	Y	(ESC I)—Moves cursor backward to typewriter tabs (Protect mode off) or to the previous start of an unprotected field (Protect mode on).
CTRL (Control)	N	N	Generates normally-nondisplayed ASCII control codes (32) when used in conjunction with another key. The control key combinations are used for special action by the terminal and/or the application program in the computer. The Control key is always used simultaneously with the other character in the command; i.e., the control key is pressed first and held down while the other key is pressed. (It is similar in action to the SHIFT key.) The commands which require simultaneous depression of two keys are indicated by a slash separating the two keys names.
ESC (Escape)	Y	N	The Escape key sends an ASCII code for Escape to the display processor. The key is generally used to momentarily leave (escape) an application program in order to use a special feature or function. Another function of the Escape key causes the next control character entered to be displayed on the screen. This facilitates putting control characters on the screen instead of going into Monitor mode. LOC ESC—When pressed in combination with SHIFT, the ESC key operates only locally to invoke the terminal functions and special features of the 925. It causes the next character entered to be interpreted as a command. The Escape key is used in conjunction with one alphanumeric character in the command sequence, i.e., the Escape key is pressed and released before the second key is pressed.

Key			Description
RETURN/ENTER	Y	Y/N	(CTRL/M)—The RETURN and ENTER keys perform the same function. They send the ASCII code (0D) for a carriage return (CR) to the display or computer. Depending on the communication mode used, the code causes the terminal to transmit a CR to the computer and/or the cursor to be moved to the first unprotected positio If the entire current line is protected, the code moves the cursor to the next unprotected position on the page. The 925 features an auto wraparound function which eliminates the need to manually enter a carriage return and a linefeed at the end of each 80-character line.
HOME	N	Y/N	(CTRL/^)—Moves cursor to first unprotected character position on the page [usually Column One of row (Line) One].
LINEFEED	Y	Y	(CTRL/J)—The LINEFEED key sends an ASCII code (0AH) for a linefeed (LF) to the computer. The code causes the terminal to transmit an LF code to the computer and the cursor to be moved down one line on the screen in half duplex, or echoed by the computer in full duplex.
BACKSPACE←	Y	Y/N	(CTRL/H)—Moves cursor one character to the left.
←	Y	Y/N	(CTRL/K)—Moves cursor up one line.
→	Y	Y/N	(CTRL/V)—Moves cursor down one line. If the cursor is on the bottom line of the screen, the display will roll up one line. If the cursor is on the bottom line of the page, the code has no effect.
↑	Y	Y/N	(CTRL/L)—Moves cursor one character to the right.
DEL (Delete)	Y	Y	The DEL key sends an ASCII DEL character to the computer portion of the 925. The computer echoes the code back to the 925 to be performed. This is usually interpreted by the 925 as a character erase code.
BREAK	N	Y	Transmits a 250-millisecond ASCII Break pulse to the computer.
Clear Space	Y	Y/N	Replaces all unprotected characters on the page with spaces. When pressed the same time as SHIFT (ESC *), it clears the entire page to nulls and turns off Protect and Half Intensity modes.
Print Key See Section 4.12 for print functions.	N	Y/N	PRINT causes all data on a page from the home position to the cursor position to be output through the printer port. The data is output with a CR, LF, and null automatically inserted at the end of each 80-character line. When Print is pressed at the same time as SHIFT, the time of day followed by a CR LF and dat
			Although escape sequences appear here with a space before the alphanumeric character, this space is *not* to be entered as part of the sequence. It is included only for the sake of clarity.

TABLE 2-1 (*Con't.*)

Key Name	Transmitted? (Yes/No)	Repeat Action? Description
Send Key	Y/N	N — Data may be sent to a computer from the 925 by several methods. When SEND is pressed, the terminal transmits all data on the page from home through the cursor position. When SEND is pressed the same time as SHIFT, the terminal transmits all data on the present line from the first column through the cursor positi See Section 3.5 for send routines.
"FUNCT" Key	Y	N — The FUNCT key transmits a user-selected character bracketed by CTRL/A (01H) and Carriage Return (CR). See Section 3.2 for FUNCT key.
F1-F11 Function Keys	Y	N — The function keys, F1 through F11, in conjunction with SHIFT key provide 22 special keys that, when pressed, transmit a 3-code sequence to your computer. When received by your computer this sequence may initiate a special form or subroutine in the program that causes the 925 to display or perform a particular fu See Section 3.1 for function keys.
Set-Up/No Scroll	Y/N	N — The No Scroll key stops screen updating during normal operation. When pressed, the 925 stops updating the screen. When pressed again, the 925 starts updating the screen. If the receive buffer fills up while update is disabled, X-Off will be sent to the computer, causing it to stop sending data. When update is reenabled, the buffer will empty, causing X-On to be sent and data to be transmitted to the computer. During normal operation, the No-Scroll function of the Set-Up/No Scrol The Set-Up key manually displays and changes the 925's operating characteristics. The set-up function is enabled by pressing Shift and Set-Up/No Scroll at the same time.
Character Insert	Y/N	Y — The Character Insert key (ESC Q) enters a space at the cursor position, causing all succeeding characters to shift one position to the right. All characters shifted past the 80th character will be lost.

	Y/N		
Character Delete	Y/N	Y	The Character Delete key (ESC W) deletes the character at the cursor position and causes all succeeding characters to shift one position to the left. All characters shifted to the cursor position will be deleted.
Line Insert/Delete	Y/N	Y	The Line Insert (ESC E) key creates an entire line of space characters on the cursor line. The data on the cursor line and all following lines shift down one line (the last line on the page is lost). The Line Delete (ESC R) causes the entire line at the cursor position to be deleted. All following lines shift up one line.
Line Erase & Page Erase	Y/N	N	Line Erase (ESC T) and Page Erase (ESC Y) replace the unprotected data (from the cursor to the end of the line or page) with a space of the proper intensity. When the keys are pressed at the same time as SHIFT, they cause a line erase to null (ESC t) or a page erase to null (ESC y).

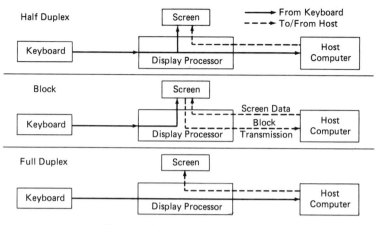

Figure 2–2 Communication Modes

2.2 BASIC OPERATIONS

This section describes various options available to you as you use the terminal:

- Setting up the terminal.
- Editing data
- Tab controls
- Emulating Tele Video 912 and 920 terminals
- Communicating with your computer system
- Printing

2.2.1 Emulations

The 925 has the capability of emulating the Tele Video 912 and 920 terminals. All control codes for this emulation can be found in Section 3.

3.1 FUNCTION KEYS

The Model 925 has the ability to transmit special function codes to your computer. This is possible through the eleven function keys located on the keyboard (Figure 2–1).

Operation of these keys (F1 through F11) causes the following three-code sequence to be transmitted. When the shift key is used in addition to the function keys, the following three-code sequence is transmitted.

To change the default value of the function keys, the system ROM of the 925 must be replaced with a modified 2732 EPROM.

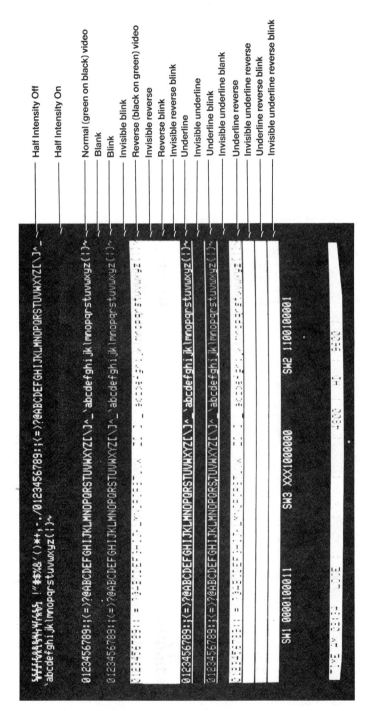

Figure 3–1 Model 925 Video Attributes

167

Key	Unshifted Code			Shifted Code		
F1	CTRL/A	@	CR	CTRL/A	`	CR
F2	CTRL/A	A	CR	CTRL/A	a	CR
F3	CTRL/A	B	CR	CTRL/A	b	CR
F4	CTRL/A	C	CR	CTRL/A	c	CR
F5	CTRL/A	D	CR	CTRL/A	d	CR
F6	CTRL/A	E	CR	CTRL/A	e	CR
F7	CTRL/A	F	CR	CTRL/A	f	CR
F8	CTRL/A	G	CR	CTRL/A	g	CR
F9	CTRL/A	H	CR	CTRL/A	h	CR
F10	CTRL/A	I	CR	CTRL/A	i	CR
F11	CTRL/A	J	CR	CTRL/A	j	CR

3.2 FUNCT (FUNCTION) KEY

Not to be confused with the Function keys (3.1), the FUNCT key transmits a user-selected character bracketed by Control A (SOH) and a Carriage Return (CR). For example, if a Control A C CR sequence is required for a special operation in a text editing program, pressing FUNCT and C at the same time transmits CONTROL A C CR to the computer automatically.

3.3 TABS

3.3.1 Setting Tabs (ESC 1)

When the Protect mode is on, the ESC 1 code generates a vertical column of half intensity spaces from the cursor position down to the first write-protected character or to the end of the page, whichever is first.

When the Protect mode is off, the code sets a typewriter-style column tab.

3.3.2 Using Tabs

3.3.2.1. Typewrite Tab (Protect and Unprotect) (CTRL/I)   When the Protect mode is off, the code causes the cursor to advance through the next typewriter-style tab set. If no tabs are set, the code has no effect and the cursor will not move.

When the Protect mode is set, the cursor is moved to the first unprotected character following the next protected field.

3.3.2.2. Field Tab (Protect only) (ESC i)   With the Protect mode set, the cursor moves exactly as described for CTRL/I, above.

With the Protect mode off, this code has no effect.

3.3.2.3.   Back Tab (ESC I)   When the Protect mode is off, the code causes the cursor to back to the previous tab position set. If no tabs are set or if the cursor is on the first tab position, Back Tab moves the cursor to the first column on the line.

If the Protect mode is on, Back Tab moves the cursor back to the start of the first preceding unprotected field. If no preceding positions exist, the cursor will not move.

If the cursor is at the first unprotected position on the page, the code has no effect. If no protected fields exist, Home position is considered the start of an unprotected field.

3.4 EDITING CONTROL

3.4.1 Set Duplex Edit Mode (ESC I)

Sets the edit keys to operate in the mode set for the alphanumeric keys. For example, if the terminal is set for Half-Duplex operation, the alphanumeric keys operate in Half Duplex mode, and the edit keys operate in Half Duplex mode.

3.4.2 Normal and Reverse Linefeed

The linefeed control code sequences and a description of their functions follow:

Linefeeds received by the Model 925 under certain conditions may result in the loss of data. Read the following control code explanations carefully!

* Linefeed (CTRL/J or LINEFEED)—with Auto Page and the Protect mode off, a linefeed advances the cursor to the next line of the page. If the cursor is at the bottom of the screen, linefeeds cause the display to roll up one line for each linefeed. If the cursor is also at the bottom of the page, a linefeed causes a new line of data to appear at the bottom of the screen and results in the loss of the top line of data on the page. The new line contains spaces. Shifted ↓ causes a linefeed.

  With the Protect mode off or on and Auto Page on, linefeed advances the cursor to the next line on the page. When it reaches the bottom of the page, it advances to the first line of the next page. When it reaches the last line of the last page, it advances to the first line of page 0.

  With the Protect mode on and Auto Page off, the cursor advances to the top of the current page when it reaches the bottom of the page.

* Reverse linefeed (ESC j)—Moves the cursor up one line for each reverse linefeed received. If the Protect mode is on and Auto Page is off, the cursor stops when it reaches the top line of the page. If Auto Page is on and the Protect mode is on or off, the cursor moves to the last line of the previous

page when it reaches the first line of the current page. If the cursor is at line 1 of page 0, it will not move.

If the Protect mode and Auto Page are off, the screen will scroll down one line when the cursor reaches the top line of the screen. If the cursor is also at the top of the page, the page will scroll down one line, causing a new line of data to appear at line 1 of the screen and deleting the last line of the current page. Shift ↑ causes a reverse linefeed.

3.5 SEND FUNCTION

3.5.1 Send Page All (ESC 7)

Sends all data on the page from Home through the cursor position. It also sends the start-protected field delimiters at the start and end, respectively, of each protected field. If the character at the cursor position is protected, the 925 sends an end-protected field delimiter to the computer. This code also sends the end-of-text character at the end of the send transmission.

3.5.2 Send Message Unprotected (ESC S)

Sends all unprotected data bracketed by the state of text (STX) and end of text (ETX) codes displayed on a page. After the data is sent, the 925 positions the cursor at the ETX code. If the page contains no STX codes, transmission begins from Home. If the page contains no ETX code, the 925 sends to the end of the page and positions the cursor at Home after the data is sent. If the page contains neither an STX nor an ETX code, the entire page will be sent. The code sends field delimiters in place of protected fields. It also sends line delimiters at the end of each line and an end-of-text delimiter at the end of the send transmission.

3.5.3 Send Message All (ESC s)

Operates in the same manner as ESC S, except that protected fields delimited by start-protected field and end-protected field are also transmitted.

3.6 TERMINATION CHARACTER SELECTION

At the completion of each send sequence, a Carriage Return (CR) is sent to the computer. This termination character may be changed to any ASCII code. To change the termination character, enter

ESC × 4NN

where NN = any two ASCII characters

Example: To change the termination character to an ETX enter

CTRL/@ (NULL)   CTRL/C (ETX)

For NN, two characters must be entered. Use a NULL (CTRL/A) as a filter code.

• Line Terminator—at the end of each line a US (1FH) is transmitted. To change the line termination character, enter

ESC × 1NN

where NN = any two ASCII characters.

3.7 PRINT FUNCTION PROGRAMMING

3.7.1 Send Time of Day

The 925 has a built in clock which keeps track of the time of day. To transmit the time to your printer, press the PRINT key in conjunction with the SHIFT key. The time will then be transmitted to the printer followed by a CR/LF and data.

3.7.2 Printer Termination Character

The printer's termination character may be reprogrammed to any character desired. To program the termination character, use the following dialogue.

ESC pn

Example: To program a null for the termination character, type:

ESC p CTRL/@

The default printer termination character is an ACK (CTRL/F).

3.8 TIME OF DAY CLOCK

The 925 has a time of day clock. The time of day will appear only when the status line is displayed during Set-Up mode. It will appear in the first field of the Status Line as follows:

TIME A(AM) P(PM)   XX(HOUR):XX(MINUTES)

To change the time, enter

ESC SPACE 1 N HH MM

where   N   = A(AM) or P(PM)
        HH = 2 digit number for the hour
        MM = 2 digit number for the minutes

Example:

If you wish to program 3 o'clock in the afternoon, enter

ESC SPACE (SPACE BAR 20H) 1 P 0300

The time of day may be sent to the printer for reports; see Section 3.7.1, print functions.

The computer may request the time from the 925 by sending the following sequence:

ESC SPACE 2

The 925 will respond with a 6-character code (A or P, hour and minutes and CR).

3.9 KEYBOARD KEYCLICK

The Model 925 features an audible keyclick whenever a key on the keyboard is depressed. The keyclick may be disabled either through a switch or software control.

        Keyclick ON   ESC >
        Keyclick OFF   ESC <

3.10 DISABLING THE KEYBOARD

You can disable all keyboard functions by remote commands from the computer. Once the keyboard is disabled, it can only be enabled once again by another remote command from the computer.

If your computer system echoes all codes, the keyboard may be accidentally disabled.

To disable the keyboard remotely, enter

ESC #

While the keyboard is disabled, all keys are disabled except FUNCT, PRINT, BREAK.

To subsequently enable it, you must receive an ESC '' from the computer or type a SHIFT/BREAK BREAK (reset) from the keyboard.

3.11 PAGE CONTROL

The Model 925 has the option of two 24-line pages of display memory. These pages may be incremented foward or backward, one page at a time. When the next page or previous page is called to the screen, the cursor assumes the last position previously occupied on that page. To control the paging functions, enter the following codes in the exact sequence shown below.

Do not enter the spaces between the characters; spaces are for clarity only.

Advance page	ESC K	(advances to next page)
Back page	ESC J	(displays previous page)
Print page and display next page	ESC P	(sends current page data to the printer and displays the second page)
Auto flip on	ESC v	(When the cursor is advanced past the 24th line, 80th character, the 925 will flip on to the next page.)
Auto flip off	ESC w	(When the cursor is advanced past the 24th line, 80th character, the cursor will move to the HOME position.)

3.12 USER LINE

3.12.1 To Load the User Line

Enter,

ESC f . . . CR

where . . . = data to appear in the user line up of 79 characters.
To cause your entry to be displayed, enter

ESC g

(You can enter data and display it later or you may display the blank User Line before entering data. This allows you to see the data as it is loaded.)

The cursor will not enter the User Line while you are inputting data.

3.12.2 Entering Data

You can enter up to 79 characters of text on the User Line. Press RETURN to terminate entry of the user message.

The User Line will be cleared when power is turned off or an ESC h is received.

3.13 CURSOR ATTRIBUTES

The cursor display may appear any one of five ways. To set the cursor display, enter the control code for the desired attribute. Type the code in the exact sequence shown below (do not enter the spaces between the characters; spaces are for clarity only):

3.14 SCREEN OFF

Attribute	Code
Not Displayed	ESC.0
Blinking Block	ESC.1
Steady Block	ESC.2
Blinking Underline	ESC.3
Steady Underline	ESC.4

To blank the entire screen, enter ESC O
  To return the screen to normal display, enter ESC N

PREVENTIVE MAINTENANCE

4.1 CARE

Tender loving care will prolong the useful life of your terminal. Clean and inspect it periodically.

4.1.1 Cleaning

To clean the terminal exterior:

1. Vacuum the keyboard every three months with a soft brush attachment (or use a small soft brush).
2. Clean the housing with a soft, lint-free cloth and a commercial detergent every three months.
   DO NOT use solvent-based or abrasive cleaners.

4.1.2 Inspection

	Description	Frequency
1.	Inspect the terminal cabinet for cracks or breaks.	1/Yr.
2.	Check each key for free movement.	1/Yr.
3.	Check the cable connector (at the rear of the terminal cabinet) for damage.	1/Yr.

TROUBLESHOOTING AND REPAIR

5.1 TROUBLESHOOTING

Your computer terminal is just one of several components in the computer system. A failure anywhere else in the system can cause the improper operation of the terminal. The computer system, memory systems, cables, modems, and operational procedures should be checked if there has been a malfunction. Table 5–1 will be helpful in determining the cause of a problem. If this table does not help locate the cause of the problem, run the self test or call a qualified service technician for assistance.

5.2 REPAIR

Model 925 operation repair is limited to changing the line fuse and the two internal power supply fuses.

5.2.1 Changing the Line Fuse

To change the line fuse, proceed as follows:
To avoid electrical shock, disconnect the terminal power cord before changing the line fuse.

1. Disconnect the terminal power cord from primary power.
2. Remove the fuse holder (see Figure 1–2) by unscrewing it counterclockwise.
3. Remove the blown fuse and replace it with a 3AG, 1 amp "slo blo" 125V or 0.5 amp, 250V fuse for 220 VAC applications instantaneous (fast blow) fuse.
4. Install the fuse in the reverse order of Steps 1 through 3.

5.2.2 Changing the Power Supply Fuses

The terminal power supply fuses are installed in fuse clips on the power supply assembly inside the terminal. To replace either of these fuses, proceed as follows:
Hazardous voltages are exposed in the cabinet. Turn off the power switch and disconnect power *before* opening the terminal cabinet.

1. Disconnect the terminal power cord from primary power.
2. Turn the terminal upside down and set it on a soft surface to prevent marring the cabinet. Remove the four Phillips screws that hold the cabinet cover on the terminal.

TABLE 3–1 TROUBLESHOOTING TERMINAL PROBLEMS

Symptom	Possible Cause	Solution
Terminal dead (no beep; no cursor)	No AC power	Plug in power cord. Turn on power switch. Check 115/230 power switch setting.
Terminal dead; cursor may appear	Loose or defective line or power supply fuses	Turn terminal power off and change fuses.
Terminal will not go on line	System is not "up."	Check status of system.
	Loose, unconnected, or damaged cables	Attach all cables and check for cable damage. Check main port (P3) interface cable pins: • 5,6, and 8 must be driven by + 12 VDC or not connected at all for normal operation. • 1 and 7 must be grounded. • 3 must be connected to the host transmitter. • 2 must be connected to the host receiver.
	Modem not turned on, defective, or phone handset on modem upside down	Turn on modem. Attach different modem. Check phone handset position.
Cursor will not appear	Defective contrast pot Contrast set too light	Refer to technical representative for adjustment of contrast settings.
System does not respond while on line	Incorrect parity switch setting, word structure, stop bits	Set parity switch to match system.
Terminal is not responding to settings	Terminal not powered down after being reconfigured; software has not scanned new settings.	Power down terminal and turn back on.
Terminal "locked up"	System is not responding; communication link is broken	Set to half duplex and try to type. If terminal will type, check cables, modem, phone lines, and computer system. Set to full duplex and perform self test.
	Terminal incorrectly set for on line and full duplex	Set to half duplex.

Symptom	Probable Cause	Corrective Action
Terminal locked up	Keyboard disabled from computer	Enter ESC"
	Switches set incorrectly	Review Chapter 2 switch settings carefully and check all switch settings.
Terminal prints correct data only part of the time	Parity settings incorrect	Check parity settings with system requirements.
	Stop bits or word structure wrong	Change switch settings.
Display is wavy	Hertz setting incorrect; does not match local power frequency	Change switch setting.
Printer does not print what is transmitted	Correct print mode selected?	Refer to Table 1-1.
	Cable connector pins connected incorrectly	Check printer port (P4) interface cable connector pins:
		• 4 or 20 must be driven by + 12 VDC or not connected at all for normal operation.
		• 3 must be connected to printer data input.
		Check other printer port device requirements.
Escape and control codes do not function as specified	The escape and/or control codes being used are not correct	Check model number of terminal and code table for correct model of terminal being used.
		Make sure upper and lower case codes are used. Is a numeral one required instead of lowercase "L"?
	Keyboard locked in SHIFT position (AUTO LOCK on)	Put in lower case. Disconnect computer system. Connect P3-2 to P3-3 and try in full duplex.
Terminal prints "garbage"	Improper baud rate setting	Set correct baud rate.
	Improper handshaking protocol	Check handshaking protocol requirements of system with terminal protocol.
	Defective modem	Replace modem.
	Noisy telephone lines	Check phone lines.
		Install dedicated phone lines.
	Static electricity	Check operating environment for static.
	EIA and AC power cords intermingled	Separate cables. Keep EIA cable separate from power cord to prevent noise on data line.

TABLE 3-1 (*cont.*)

Symptom	Possible Cause	Solution
Terminal prints "garbage"	AC outlet not wired properly	Check for proper wiring and grounding
Erroneous data sent to computer Scrambled output Terminal loses memory	Static electricity	1. Check operating environment for static problems. 2. Install antistatic floor mat. 3. Spray carpeting with antistatic spray. 4. Increase humidity.
	AC outlet not wired properly	Check for proper wiring and grounding.
Terminal does not print what is typed while on line	Duplex switch incorrectly set	Set duplex switch to match host system.
Terminal only prints @ characters	Word length switch set incorrectly Parity switch set incorrectly Stop bits set incorrectly	Set word length switch to match computer system. Set parity switch to match computer system. Set stop bit switch to match computer system.

3. Turn the terminal right side up and lift off the cabinet cover. Make sure there is adequate table space for the open terminal.
4. Remove the blown fuse from its fuse clip.
5. Replace the blown fuse with a 3AG, 3 amp, 125V fuse.
6. Reinstall the terminal cover and secure it with the four screws. (Do not overtighten screws!)

GLOSSARY

ASCII   The acronym for American Standard Code for Information Interchange. This is a standardized code for the transmission of data within the United States. It is composed of 128 characters (upper and lowercase letters, numerals, punctuation marks, symbols, and control characters) in a 7-bit binary format.

Asynchronous Communication   A method of communication where the time synchronization of the transmission of data between the sending and receiving stations is set by start and stop bits and the baud rate.

Baud   The rate of transmission data. One baud equals one binary bit per second.

Bit   An abbreviation for binary digit. A bit is the smallest unit of data. ASCII codes are composed of seven bits.

Break   To break or interrupt communications. When the BREAK switch on the terminal is toggled, a 250-millisecond tone is sent to the computer to immediately halt communications.

Buffer   An electronic device within the terminal that allows for the temporary storage of incoming data should the transmission rate of the incoming data be faster than the terminal's printing speed.

Bug   An error in a computer program or in the operation of the computer.

Byte   A coded group of binary bits which represents a character (letter, numeral, symbol, command, etc.).

Code   A method of representing data by groups of binary digits.

Command   A code that will cause the terminal or computer to perform an electronic or mechanical action.

Computer   An electronic system which, in accordance with its programming, will store the process information and perform high-speed mathematical or logical operations.

Control Codes   Special nonprinting codes which cause the terminal or computer to perform specific electronic or mechanical actions (such as setting tabs, etc.).

CPU   Central Processing Unit. The ''brains'' of a computer or computer terminal; that section where the logic and control functions are performed.

Default   Condition which exists from POWER ON or RESET if no instructions to the contrary are given to the terminal.

DEL   The ASCII DELETE code used in some instances to delete transmitted characters or to exit modes of operation.

Digit   One of the numerals in a number system.

Digital   Information in the form of individual parts—bits or digits.

EOT   An ASCII code that means "end of transmission" (EOT); used in the EOT/ACK handshaking protocol. The computer sends an EOT at the end of each transmission to the terminal. When the terminal is ready to receive more data, it transmits an acknowledge (ACK) back to the computer.

ESC   An ASCII code meaning "escape" which is used to control various electronic and mechanical functions of the terminal.

Full Duplex   In full duplex communication, the terminal can transmit and receive *simultaneously*. The transmitted data is not printed locally unless it is "echoed back" by the computer.

Half Duplex   In half duplex communication, the terminal transmits and receives data in separate, *consecutive operations*. Transmitted data is printed locally.

Handshaking   A communications protocol which is necessarily used when the transmitting speed of the computer is faster than the printing speed of the terminal. It consists of a set of commands, recognized by both stations, which control the flow of the data transmission from the computer.

Hardware   The electronic components of a computer system or terminal.

Host   The computer system.

Interface   A communciations channel which is typically used for external devices.

Main   The computer system.

Memory   That part of a computer system or terminal where information is stored.

Microprocessor   An electronic circuit on the surface of a small silicon chip which can be programmed to perform a wide variety of functions within the computer system or terminal.

Modem   An electronic device which converts (modulates) the serial communications between the computer and terminal into audible tones which can be transmitted over telephone lines. All received data is reconverted (demodulated) from the audible tones into serial information.

NUL   An ASCII code ("nothing") which is used as a fill character in some communications formats.

Parity   A method of checking for errors in data communications. An extra bit (either a "1" or "0"), called the parity bit, is added to the end of each ASCII character to make the final count of ''1'' bits in the character an even or odd number, according to a prearranged format. Some systems always use even parity, some always use odd parity, and some do not check for parity. Both terminal and system *must* be set for the same parity.

Protocol   All of the conventions which must be observed in order for the computer and terminal to communicate with each other.

Serial Communication   The standard method of ASCII character transmission where bits are sent, one at a time, in sequence. Each 7-bit ASCII character is preceded by a start bit (see Asynchronous Communication) and ended with a parity bit and stop bit.

Toggle   Activation or deactivation of function or mode key (either a receive key, command sequence, or manual keystroke).

Wraparound   Movement of the cursor as it reaches the right edge of screen, disappears, and ''wraps around'' to the beginning of the next line.

X-ON/X-OFF   A handshaking protocol. When the terminal's buffer is nearly full, it transmits an X-OFF to the computer to stop transmission; when the buffer is almost empty, an X-ON is transmitted to the host to resume transmission.

Index